Ready, Set, Grow!

BURPEE®

Ready, Set, Grow!

a guide to gardening
with children

Suzanne Frutig Bales

BURPEE®

Macmillan • USA

MACMILLAN
A Simon & Schuster Macmillan Company
1633 Broadway
New York, NY 10019-6785

Library of Congress Cataloging-in-Publication Data

Bales, Suzanne Frutig.
Ready, set, grow : a guide to gardening with children /Suzanne Frutig Bales.
p.   cm.
Includes index.
ISBN 0-02-860399-0
1. Children's gardens.   2. Gardening.   3. Flower arrangement.   4. Nature craft.   I. Title.
SB457.B265   1996
635—dc20   95-39008
CIP

All photos are by the author except for the following:
W. Atlee Burpee & Co.: pp. 11, 12, 14, 83, 86, 94, 100, 101, 103, 105, 117 (*both*), 118
Bridget Flint: pg. 51 (*lower right*)
Martha Kraska: pp. 87, 88, 110
Netherland Flower Bulb Information Center: pg. 15
H. Ross: pg. 122

Design by Vertigo Design
Illustrations by Alison Lew
Additional Illustrations by Rachel McBrearty

Manufactured in the United States of America
10 9 8 7 6 5 4 3 2 1

*Page iii: In the hands of children,
a wheelbarrow has many imaginative uses.*

*Page v: Sharing a garden with a child at a young age is the start
of a life-long interest.*

This book is dedicated to the children of Graham-Windham. It is inspiring to see what they have achieved.

Never underestimate the
joy of a harvest.

Acknowledgments

I would like to express my gratitude to the many people who have helped me. Again, as in my other books, I have to thank my father, Ed Frutig, who graciously gave freely of his time to help me shape and edit the book. My thanks go to my husband and best friend Carter, my gardening partner Martha Kraska, and my assistant Gina Norgard for providing me with unending help and support. Many thanks to my neighbor and close friend Carol Schmidlapp, and her wonderful children who helped me test various garden activities. The American Horticulture Society Children's Symposiums, the Netherlands Flower Bulb Information Center, Sally Ferguson in particular, and the 4-H Youth Program bulletins written by Jane L. Taylor assisted me in my research. I especially want to thank Jane Taylor for sharing ideas through her writing, the children's garden at Michigan State University, and Katie Moss Warner at Disney World's Children's garden. Both were inspirational.

At W. Atlee Burpee & Co., I would like to thank Barbara Wolverton and Elda Malgieri.

Thanks go to all of the children whose pictures appear in the book: My children, Catie and Carter Bales; my niece Abby Bales; the Schmidlapp children, Jake, Deuce and Charlotte; Katie Hirschfield; and the Frutig children, Rachel, Luke and Edward.

Contents

Introduction xi

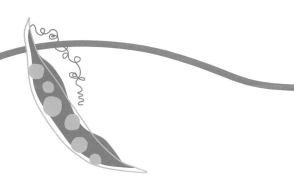

Kids' Crafts and Activities 57

4

Fun and Funny Plants 95

Index 128

Introduction

Don't fight it! Kids love digging in the dirt.

Gardening introduces children to a love of common things and experiences in their environment. Gardens are a source of wonderful childhood memories and can be a parent's greatest gift. When parents are enthusiastic, the excitement catches. Sharing a garden with children requires patience, humor and a belief in magic. We must encourage and inspire our children if we wish to hold their slippery attention. Choose the ideas from this book that interest you and your child's attention will follow.

Gertrude Jekyll wrote in *Children and Gardens* (1908), "The best way to [help children] love gardens is to give them a pretty one ready made." As the patience and attention span of young children wanes, let them come and go in the garden as they please. Allow them to mess around in the mud and get dirty, a favorite activity of children throughout the ages.

Gimmicks add an element of surprise and fun helping to capture a child's attention. In her wisdom, Mother Nature has provided many such elements. The miracle of seeds growing into giant pumpkins, soldier-high sunflowers or teeny, tiny carrots, the Jack-be-little pumpkins that fit in your hand, all tickle and excite children.

Opposite page: Luke Frutig takes great pride in his harvest of zucchini, cucumbers and beans.

Mammoth sunflowers, a favorite, germinate quickly, towering over both kids and parents in about eight weeks. Everyone cranes their neck to look up at a sunflower's face. And as a bonus, there are numerous ways to use the sunflower seeds. They can be picked, dried, roasted, shelled and eaten, or fed to birds (see page 125).

The skills needed for growing a garden are in the Ready, Set, Grow! chapter beginning on page 1. There are also indoor projects for city gardeners such as starting seeds indoors, or forcing bulbs to bloom. The most fun for children occurs when they see seedlings pop out of the soil or bulbs bloom for the first time (see pages 15–17).

In the Gardens Designed for Kids chapter, there are assorted garden plans simple enough for older children to follow or for parents to plant for younger children to enjoy. The plans include a tepee garden (see pages 42–43), a sunflower house and a garden to attract butterflies (pages 44–47).

The Fun and Funny Plants chapter emphasizes the quick and easy to grow, as well as the strange and weird plants that are Mother Nature's children. They are selected to engage any child's attention. Suggestions are given for growing huge pumpkins, ugly pocked gourds and beautiful, but bizarre strawflowers. Kids can watch the scarlet flowers of the runner bean change and grow into mature beans, pick them, and be surprised when they open the green pod to find bright neon-pink beans (see page 98). Flowers not only fascinate children by their appearance, but also by their feel and smell. Encourage children to touch plants, gently of course, and to smell their flowers. Introduce them to the pleasures of picking and eating fruits and vegetables right from the vine. *Cockscomb celosia*, for example, comes in neon colors and feels like crushed velvet. Lamb's ears foliage, true to its namesake, looks and feels like the ears of a lamb. And everlasting flowers are papery to the touch, come in bright colors and last all winter in arrangements

Edward enjoys tiny tomatoes right from the vine.

without water (see pages 68–70). Nasturtiums smell peppery, and roses, depending on the variety, can smell sweet, fruity, spicy or even like a fresh-brewed cup of tea.

There is a wide range of garden activities to do with children. Both simple and complex activities are included in the Kids' Crafts and Activities Chapter to interest young children as well as teenagers. The activities and crafts were selected because they are fun as well as educational. It is no secret that everyone learns more when they enjoy what they are doing. Many of the projects, such as candying flowers, tattooing a pumpkin, pressing flowers and picking bouquets can be done by young children with the help of an adult or a teenager alone. The pictures that follow are a good starting place to see what interests them.

I have added some of my favorite garden elements, the most popular being scarecrows. They really do not work to keep birds and animals out of the garden, but they do give personality and visitors a chuckle. Children enjoy dressing them, naming them, and even talking to them (see pages 58–63). Let the kids name the garden and make signs—like those in the Michigan State 4-H Children's Garden that say "Please Touch."

The wildlife in a garden has also been included as an important part of getting to know and understand the garden environment. It is a source of interest to children from the "ugh" reserved for slugs to the "oohs" for butterflies. Hopping after toads if you're lucky enough to have them (they help control your insect population), or even picking or flicking slow-moving caterpillars and Japanese beetles off leaves into a bottle of water, are educational activities for children and should be encouraged. Order friendly, beneficial insects and earthworms through the mail and let your children release them in the garden to help control harmful insects (see pages 28–30). After all, a garden is a wonderful thing to share with children—yours, your neighbors' and those of your friends.

Jake and Larry Schmidlapp are collecting
the seeds of love-in-a-puff from the climbing
vine. Jake is surprised that Mother Nature
decorated the black seeds with tiny white hearts.

1

ready, set,
grow!

seeds

The promise of a seed is the miracle of life in an assortment of different colors, sizes and shapes. A single seed can be as large as a coconut or as small as dust. Tiny begonia seeds are counted under a microscope. However, the seeds you are probably most familiar with are the brown oval seeds inside an apple and the white seeds in oranges. The black, flat seeds in watermelon are almost as well known.

Pictured here are the seeds and flowers of red celosia, yellow black-eyed Susan, pink cleome, blue bachelor's buttons, double red impatien, yellow marigold, the brown and green seed pods of love-in-a-mist, sunflowers and love-in-a-puff (center) with white hearts on each black seed.

Place a seed in your child's hand and let the child ponder for a moment. Explain that each seed, little or big, has all the nutrients necessary to sprout and grow to a thousand times its size, lacking only moisture to wake from its dormant state. It is unbelievably sturdy and self-sufficient.

To show a child how a seed sprouts from the food and nutrients already stored inside it, completely wet a paper towel, wring it out and lay it flat. Distribute some bean seeds on the paper towel. Roll up the towel loosely and place it in a warm location. Open the towel in a few days and you will have sprouted seeds.

Another easy experiment to do with children is to grow an avocado plant. An avocado pit, the seed of the avocado, will grow with only its bottom touching water. Insert three toothpicks evenly spaced around the middle of the avocado pit. Place the avocado pit pointed end up and suspend it above the rim of a glass or jar. Fill the jar with water so that the bottom half of the pit is covered. When roots and leaves appear, plant the seed, half buried, in a small pot filled with potting soil. Place it in a sunny window and keep the soil damp. As the stem and leaves grow upward, pinch off the small leaves at the top to force the avocado to branch out and become a bushy green houseplant.

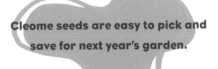
Cleome seeds are easy to pick and save for next year's garden.

the way seeds travel

When they are ripe, seeds have to be touching soil in a place where they can grow. If all seeds merely dropped to the ground near the mother plant, there wouldn't be enough room for all of them to grow. Plants spread their seeds in many different ways: Some fly, some are carried, some shoot their seeds into the air, and others hitchhike.

Who can resist making a wish and blowing on a dandelion puff to watch it glide on the breeze? I can't. The dandelion is the best known and the most widely grown of the seeds that take flight. The seeds of thistles are also great navigators. They have parachutes to catch the wind and ride high on the breeze. Seeds of some trees, such as maples, elms and ash, have flat, enlarged oval wings that look like airplane propellers, allowing them to glide through the air.

Animals, birds and bats eat berries with seeds hidden inside, providing another means of transport. The seeds pass through their bodies unharmed and germinate where they land. Heavier seeds such as acorns fall from trees and are transported by squirrels, mice and birds to new places. Rain water, especially when it forms rivulets running off sloping hills, also carries seeds to new places. People, of course, as they move from place to place, have carried their favorite seeds with them.

Some plants, impatiens and spider flowers, for example, shoot their seeds through the air when they are ripe. As each seedpod ripens, it bursts and catapults the seeds away from the plant. Anyone may trigger the seedpod by gently pressing it when ripe.

4

Tools

Adult gardening tools are often awkward and heavy for young children. Children can be defeated early if their hands can't fit around the rake or shovel. Having their own child-size garden tools, including a wheelbarrow, helps give children pride in the garden. There are many child-size tools available for younger children and lightweight tools in adult sizes available for older children. A list of appropriate tools for children include:

A TROWEL
A HOE
A SHOVEL
A WHEELBARROW
A RAKE
AN APRON
GARDENING GLOVES
A HAT
ROUNDED SCISSORS

Outfitted, carefully supervised children will be ready for fun in the garden.

Having the proper child-size tools will make it easier for a child to garden. Catie holds up her garden gloves (left) and shows off her wheelbarrow (above).

Other seeds hitchhike, traveling in burs and catching rides on the fur of animals or the clothes of people until they are rubbed or scratched off in a new place. Next time you walk through the woods or the tall grass in a meadow, check your socks and pant legs to see if you have caught any burs. When they touch your skin they itch and prickle. Dogs and other long-haired animals have a hard time ridding themselves of stubborn burs, making them an excellent means of seed transportation.

Look in your garden to see what seeds you can collect to plant next summer. Historically, an important part of pilgrim family gardens was a small area where one or two plants of each vegetable were allowed to go to seed to provide for next year's crops.

Marigolds are among the easiest to collect as they hold their seeds in tight bundles pointed up. Commercial seed companies now have trucks that ride over plant rows and vacuum up the seeds. If you grow marigolds, leave a few flowers to go to seed. Tomatoes and melons are more difficult to collect. They have to be squashed and the seeds removed from the pulp, washed and dried. Store each different seed type in separate plastic sandwich bags in a cool, dark place. Make sure the seeds are dry before closing the bag, as high heat and a damp quarters will create mold and ruin the seeds.

making your bed

When preparing a new garden bed, keep in mind the plants want the same things you do; a comfortable bed, nutritious food, clean water, fresh air, shelter from strong wind, excessive cold and extreme heat.

A child's garden can be grown anywhere: in the middle of a vegetable garden, in an area of lawn where the grass has been removed or to one side of a play area. Choose a location with good drainage that receives at least six hours of direct sunshine each day. Follow the graph measurements for the plans in the next chapter, using clothesline or a garden hose to outline the garden. Try pouring a thin line of ground limestone from a pitcher to draw the outside border of the garden and the sections within it. With a spade or edging tool, cut along the marked edges. If the area is in grass, remove the sod and mix organic material such as compost and well-rotted manure into the soil. For planting and growing, always follow the directions on the seed packs.

If you are planting a traditional garden with seeds in rows, place a stick in the ground at each end of the row.

Jake turns over the soil, the first step in planting a garden.

7

Stretch a piece of string between the two sticks spanning the length of the row. The stretched string forms a straight line to follow when you plant. At one end of the row, place a plant marker to identify what seeds were planted in the row. The easiest plant marker is a stick poked through the top of the seed packet and stuck into the ground at one end of the row. Wooden or plastic plant markers can be purchased and plant names can be written in pencil or indelible ink to last a season. One

A garden can be an outdoor playroom, a place to encourage a child's imagination and a place to relax surrounded by nature's beauty.

children's garden I visited used large, flat, colorful lollipops still in their plastic wrap and with the seed names painted on them.

Do not crowd plants by planting seeds too close together. Crowding weakens the plants and results in fewer vegetables or flowers. Roots need room to spread and grow. Large seeds are easy to space correctly as they can be transferred to your hand and placed one at a time to the depth and distance advised on the packages. Tiny seeds are more difficult to spread. One way to plant them is to fold a piece of paper in half, empty your seeds into the crease, and let them fall slowly out of the crease onto the seed bed. You can also mix the tiny seeds with sand and then spread them, but to be successful make sure you use more sand than seed.

If the seeds are to be grown in clusters rather than lines, toss the seed thinly in each section, cover them with the recommended depth of fine soil and firm gently. Water with a fine spray to prevent the seeds from washing away. Keep the soil moist until the plants have emerged and become well established (7 to 21 days, depending on the type of seed, the condition of the soil, and the weather).

When the seedlings grow large enough to handle, thin them to the spacing recommended on the seed packets for each variety. You can prolong the harvest and increase the production of most flowers or vegetables by picking them regularly.

Seed Tips

1. **Air and water:** All seeds need the right combination of air and moisture to germinate. If they are too wet, sitting in a puddle or soggy soil, they are deprived of air and will rot instead of germinating. Remember to keep them damp, but not soaking wet.

2. **Temperature:** Every seed variety germinates best at a certain temperature. Most annual seeds like a temperature between 65 and 80 degrees Fahrenheit. However, some seeds prefer cooler temperatures. It is best to check each seed variety for the best growing temperature.

3. **Light or dark:** Most seeds germinate best in the dark (that is why we bury them). It is important to be aware of those seeds that require light to germinate, such as impatiens, begonias and petunias. For the seeds that require darkness, the planting depth is important. Read your seed packet and plant accurately.

4. **Days to germination:** This will tell you approximately how many days before you will see your seed sprouting. When a seed has sprouted, its requirements change. If it needed dark to germinate, it now needs light to grow. While germinating, seeds supply themselves with food; once sprouted, they need to be fed with sun, soil and moisture.

Burpee's easy-sow straight-row seed tapes

Growing from seed is easy with seed tapes. There's no need to thin out the seeds as they are already correctly spaced along 15-foot paper tapes that dissolve after planting. Each tape can be cut into different lengths for multiple row planting or they can be saved for a second sowing. It is often easier for young children to handle seed tapes rather than individual small seeds. It also reduces the time it takes to plant and eliminates the work involved in thinning the seedlings later.

Seed tapes make it easy for children to plant in straight rows with seeds properly spaced.

11

Starting Seeds Indoors

While I enjoy winter, it invariably lasts too long and I am always impatient for the arrival of spring. Starting seeds indoors lets my hands get dirty sooner and helps me realize my garden dreams earlier. It is also the perfect time to capture the kids' attention as the weather outside forces them in and the frequent refrain of "I'm bored" starts in earnest.

Starting seeds earlier indoors extends, by weeks, the length of time flowers bloom in the garden. Seedlings transplanted into the warming, frost-free garden soil flower much faster than seeds planted directly into the garden at a later date.

Seed 'n Start kits come complete with everything needed to start seeds indoors.

For all seeds, timing is important. You can plant a fast sprouting seed such as a sunflower inside just for the pleasure of watching it grow. But if you want to transplant it to the garden where it can grow tall enough to flower, plant the seed indoors about six weeks before the last frost leaves your area. If you plant seeds too early, they will grow weak and spindly, held in a pot too long before they can be planted in a frost-free garden.

There are many different kinds of equipment for seed starting. After reading the list that follows, you can easily

decide which equipment and method of growing suits you. Whichever container you use, the methods are the same. First, purchase a planting mix for the best results. It should not contain weed seed and should provide balanced nutrition. Second, saturate your planting mix so it is damp but not soggy. Let the excess water run out the bottom, but don't let the container sit in water. If your soil is too wet, your seed roots will rot. Third, let the planting mixture set a half hour or so until it becomes evenly moist before planting your seeds.

Once the seeds are in the planting mixture, cover them with a dome, or enclose the entire unit in a clear plastic bag to preserve the moisture. The bag should not be allowed to touch the soil and can be easily held up with a plant marker or a stick to create a tent. The tent acts like a greenhouse, keeping the air and soil moist and warm. Set it in a warm place out of direct sunlight. If the seeds require light, a windowsill exposed to sunlight five or six hours a day is ideal.

Check daily to assure your seeds are evenly moist. The best method of watering is to set your containers in a tray of water for a half hour until they absorb as much water as they can hold. If you are watering from the top, spray with a very delicate soft spray. Don't overwater or let water sit in puddles on top of the seed.

When seedlings appear, remove the plastic bag, and place the plants in light to avoid stem rot. If you set the plants in a window, turn them daily so they will grow straight as they reach for sunlight. An ideal seedling is straight, deep-rooted and bushy.

A SAMPLING OF SEED-STARTING CONTAINERS

Peat pots: Shaped like a small flowerpot, molded of peat and wood fiber, peat pots are filled with planting mix. Each pot is planted with three seeds and later thinned to one seedling per pot. The advantage of peat pots is that there is no disturbance to the roots as the pot is planted into the garden with the soil

Peat pots are shaped like small flowerpots while peat pellets are compressed peat that expands when watered. Both are good for growing an individual seed.

level inside the peat pot beneath the surface of your garden. Plants with delicate roots have trouble growing through the peat pot, so when planting, carefully loosen or tear the sides and bottom in a few places to allow the roots easy access to your garden's soil. Remove any of the pot's rim that protrudes above the soil level to prevent the molded peat from acting like a wick that draws water up, and dries out the roots.

Peat pellets: Peat pellets are formed from compressed peat and covered with a thin plastic net. They expand when watered, and each peat pellet supports one seedling. Like peat pots, the seedlings and pellets are planted directly into the soil.

Seed 'n Start kits: Developed by Burpee in cooperation with a leading college of agriculture, Seed 'n Start kits were designed with the home gardener in mind. Each kit consists of 10 extra-deep cells filled with Burpee's special seed-starting formula, set on a tray for easy bottom watering. A transparent dome is included to protect the seeds from drying out during germination. From start to finish they are the least complicated for children.

Household containers: You can successfully sprout seeds in old milk containers, plastic and paper cups, as well as clay pots, but be sure they are clean. Scrub them with soapy water and let them sit in a solution of one part household bleach to ten parts water for a half hour. Each container will need a drainage hole in the bottom. Fill the pot with a seed-starting soil-less mix to within $1/2$ inch of the top and plant your seeds.

bulbs

Bulbs are the garden's sleeping beauties. They are living plants, practically guaranteed to grow if you put them in the ground at the proper planting time. It is as close to a "sure thing" as a gardener ever gets. Bulbs arrive complete with a potential flower or two inside. They are well-fed, round, firmly packed and nearly foolproof. Failure is possible only if bulbs rot from being planted in swampy soil or if they are dug up and eaten by an animal such as a squirrel.

Each bulb increases by offshoots from the mother bulb. The mother bulb usually continues to live, year after year, in nutritious, well-drained soil. If you slice a daffodil vertically in half, your child can see the "baby flower" in the middle just waiting to burst forth in Spring. Also present are the embryo leaves, stems and the stored food that surrounds them. The stem starts at the bottom of the bulb and grows up through it. After blooming and while the foliage is dying back, the embryo, leaves and flower buds are formed. This is why some bulbs, like paperwhite daffodils and

Planting fall bulbs is an easy way to start a child gardening. A bulb is as close to a "sure thing" as a gardener ever gets.

15

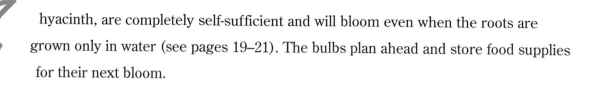

hyacinth, are completely self-sufficient and will bloom even when the roots are grown only in water (see pages 19–21). The bulbs plan ahead and store food supplies for their next bloom.

The easiest bulbs to grow are the spring bloomers—daffodils, crocus and tulips—but they should be planted in the fall. Be sure to check the planting instructions that come with your bulbs. Each has its own planting depth; daffodils and tulips are 6 to 8 inches, while crocus are 4 inches. A good rule of thumb is to plant each bulb to a depth of three times the largest diameter of the bulb.

The best and easiest way to plant bulbs is to layer them in the garden. Dig a hole the size of a dinner plate, about 9 inches deep. The soil removed from the top of the bed is the most nutritious, thus "topsoil." You want this rich soil on the bottom where the bulbs can use it, and the soil mixed with compost or shredded leaves and a sprinkling of ground limestone. This provides a nutritious bed for the roots of the bulbs.

Place six daffodils equally spaced in the hole, pointed side up. Cover the daffodils with more soil until the hole is 4 inches from the top. At this level, plant 10 to 12 grape hyacinths, also equally spaced and pointed side up. Again cover with soil and plant snowdrops on top at 2 to 3 inches from the top of the hole. Fill in the remaining space, firm the soil by gently pressing it down with your foot, fertilize with a slow-release fertilizer such as Holland Bulb Booster and gently water. Add more soil if needed.

The bulbs will bloom at different times, each only showing above the ground for a few months. They are compatible and provide a beautiful display when planted closely together. Layering bulbs also works for trench planting. You can make a crazy quilt pattern of colors or even write your children's names in different colored bulbs. And any spring bulbs could be substituted for the ones I chose. Simply check their planting guide to find the approximate planting depth. Once planted, the bulbs return year after year to bring pleasure to the whole family.

Fooling Bulbs

Most spring bulbs can be easily fooled into blooming earlier than usual. There are two methods of fooling bulbs. We can fool or force most bulbs by putting them in a refrigerator for a short period of time (8 to 12 weeks) to make them believe they have gone through a winter. Then grow them indoors on a sunny windowsill, letting them think spring has arrived. The second method, growing bulbs with their bottoms in water, is the simplest. However, it only works for crocus, hyacinths and paperwhite daffodils. Other varieties of daffodils and tulips will not bloom without soil.

FOOLING BULBS PLANTED IN SOIL

Hyacinths, amaryllises and paperwhite daffodils are perhaps the easiest to force, no matter which method is used, and tulips are the most challenging. When planting hyacinths, amaryllises and paperwhite daffodils in soil, you can skip the cooling period unless you want to hold the bulbs for later bloom. Among the tulip varieties, the easiest to force are the early singles and early doubles.

All spring-flowering bulbs should be potted in late September or early October. Fooling the bulbs, better known as forcing bulbs, takes about twelve weeks for crocus and daffodils and about sixteen weeks for tulips. By planting many kinds and carefully timing their bloom, you can have indoor color from late December through April. The quality of the bulb determines its performance when forced. Always use top-size, healthy, firm bulbs which are guaranteed to grow and bloom.

Any container from a clay pot to a china bowl works. The container must be clean and have a drainage hole. The ideal size for a container is half as high as it is wide, providing planting space for a cluster of bulbs. The size of the bulbs will determine the height of the container. If possible, plant as many bulbs as the pot will hold, leaving only a $1/2$ inch of space between the bulbs and around the edge of the pot. Spring bulbs look best when planted in groups of 6 to 12 bulbs per pot, all of the same kind or variety. Hyacinths, however, are often planted individually in 4- to 5-inch pots. Two or three large daffodil bulbs, or 6 tulip bulbs, or 12 crocus fill a 6-inch pot nicely.

Place an inch of pebbles in the bottom of the pot over the drainage hole. Half fill the pot with a good potting mix. Set the bulbs on the soil (be sure the tops are pointing up!), with the tops just below the rim of the pot; do not press the bulbs into the soil. Add soil until only the tips of the bulbs are visible. Small bulbs can be covered with $1/2$ inch of soil. Water the pot thoroughly and let the excess water drain off. Label each pot with the name of the bulb and the date it was planted.

Store the pots of bulbs immediately in a cool, dark place such as an unheated attic, porch, attached garage, cold frame or spare refrigerator. In the ideal place, the temperature will remain above freezing but not go above 45 degrees Fahrenheit. A frost-free location promotes better root development. If necessary, set boxes, pots or burlap over your potted bulbs to keep them dark during this period. Keep the soil barely damp; check periodically (every few weeks) and water only when the soil approaches dryness.

After 8 to 10 weeks of cold temperatures, the bulbs develop good roots. You will know when the bulb has good roots because it will send up top sprouts. When the top shoots are 2 to 3 inches high, move the bulbs to a sunny window. The sun forces them to bloom. (I have forgotten bulbs from time to time and brought them out when the stems were 6 inches high and a bright jaundice yellow color. They quickly recover; one day of sunlight restores their healthy green color.)

If you sprinkle grass seed on top of the soil between the tops of the bulbs, the grass germinates in a week and quickly grows to a few inches high, but it must be kept moist. The green grass completes the beauty of the blooming bulbs as it hides the bare soil.

FOOLING TO BLOOM IN WATER

Remember, only crocus, hyacinth and paperwhite daffodils will bloom with this method.

Before you start, decide when you want your bulbs to flower. Bulbs started at 10-day intervals provide a sequence of bloom for many weeks or months. Until you are ready to use them, store the bulbs in perforated paper bags and keep them in a cool, dark, dry place. The bottom shelf of a refrigerator is fine for hyacinths and crocus, but too cold for daffodils.

Paperwhite daffodils are the easiest bulbs to "fool" into blooming indoors in winter.

19

Each bulb takes a different amount of time to come into bloom. Paperwhite daffodils bloom in about 4 to 6 weeks after you start them. For Christmas bloom, start the bulbs in mid-November. Hyacinths require a longer period, about 6 to 8 weeks, to establish good roots. Crocuses need a much longer time and a more gradual transition from dark to light. They must be kept cool until their buds rise from the leaves, so do not expect flowers before the end of January if crocus bulbs are started in mid-November.

To grow bulbs in water, select a container about twice as deep as the bulbs and fill it $1/6$ to $3/4$ full with clean pebbles, marbles, gravel or coarse sand. Place the bulbs on top, and fill the container with water until it just touches the bottom of the bulbs; any higher and the bulbs will rot. (A piece of charcoal added to the water will keep it fresh.) Fill the spaces between the bulbs with added gravel and sand to hold them firmly upright.

Set the dish of bulbs in a dark, cool (50 to 60 degrees Fahrenheit), well-ventilated spot, such as a cool closet or basement, until you see a mass of roots growing between the gravel, usually within two to three weeks. Check the water level occasionally to make sure the roots are always immersed because roots will die quickly if exposed to air.

When the sprouts are 2 to 3 inches high, transfer the bulbs to a cool location with bright indirect light (such as a north window) for three or four days. Finally, move the bulbs into full sunlight. When the flowers open, you can prolong their bloom by moving the bulbs again to a cooler place out of direct sunlight. Discard the bulbs after they have bloomed. The water method zaps all their energy and they will not recover even if planted in the garden.

Daffodils and hyacinths grown by this method usually need staking to look their best when in flower. Support them with sticks inserted into the pebbles or sand, and make a fence by looping string loosely around each of the sticks, connecting the sticks to each other several times.

Hyacinths and crocuses may also be grown by simply suspending the bulb in a glass of water. Specially designed glasses for these bulbs are available, but you may use any tapered glass or jar that holds the bulb above the water. Fill the glass so the water just touches the bottom of the bulb. Change the water when it starts to discolor, usually every couple of weeks, taking care to maintain the correct water level as bulbs will die very quickly when their roots are exposed to air. Keep the bulbs in a cool, dark place until the lower portion of the glass fills with roots, then move it gradually into greater light and warmth. Discard the bulb after flowering.

Childproofing and Yard-Safety Tips for Gardening with Children

With the right attitude, the garden and yard, just like a properly childproofed home, can be a safe and happy place for family fun in all seasons.

1. The number one rule for children in the garden is to never eat anything unless an adult is supervising. While eating fruits and vegetables you've grown yourself is part of the joy of gardening, many common ornamental plants can make you quite sick if you eat them; some are very poisonous.

2. Never leave a toddler or young child outside unattended.

3. Point out any potential hazards to the child, such as thorn bushes or poison ivy. Fence off areas of plants that should be avoided, if necessary.

4. Be careful with sharp tools and discuss with your children which tools are safe for them to use and which are not. Place forks, rakes and other pointed tools points down.

5. No chemicals. Despite their sometimes colorful labels, garden chemicals are highly dangerous if mishandled and have no place in a garden with young children. A child's garden, above all other, should be an organic garden. If you do have garden chemicals, be sure to store them in clearly marked containers, perhaps with a big skull and crossbones. Never use soft drink bottles or other empty food containers for storing chemicals, cleaning supplies or fertilizers.

6. Always wash your hands after gardening.

The above tips on outdoor safety with children are from the Netherlands Flower Bulb Information Center.

mother nature's
mysteries and magic
(a section for kids of all ages)

Insects, like people, are a mixture—some good, some bad. Insects can be so beautiful they make you smile or so ugly, they make you squirm. Remember, most insects don't sting, bite or destroy things.

There are more kinds of insects than all other varieties of animals and plants combined. Three out of every four animals are insects. What sets insects apart from other animals is their lack of bones. Instead they have tough skin and strong muscles.

Insects populated the earth even before the dinosaurs. It looks like they'll be with us forever, so we need to get to know and understand them. Like people, they are a mixed group that include the good, the bad and the ugly. The good are necessary for our existence. They should always be welcome in your garden, for they are Nature's way of controlling pests. So let's get to know "who's who" in the insect kingdom.

23

Catie is releasing the ladybugs she ordered through the mail. They will help keep the "bad" bugs from eating her plants.

Be a Bug Detective

See what bugs you can detect in your yard or even your house. To be a bug detective, all you need is a magnifying glass, a butterfly net and a jar with a few small air holes punched in the lid. The butterfly net can be used to catch many of the flying insects, and crawling insects can be flicked into the jar.

A magnifying glass will let you look closer at the leaves of plants, especially their underside where bugs hide and go undetected. Bugs that are easy to catch can be left in a jar for a short time to examine up close. But only catch bugs you know will not sting and release butterflies after a short time so they will not die.

LADYBUGS

The ladybug may be the greatest asset to any garden. She is certainly among the smallest. Yet each day a ladybug eats many times her own weight in aphids, mealybugs, leafhoppers, fleas, lice and other garden pests in their egg and larval stages before they can destroy healthy plants. Ladybugs are beautiful with their red dresses and black polka dots (a hard body covering) artfully hiding two wings that carry the ladybug away when it detects trouble. If you see one on a leaf and put your finger near it, often a ladybug will climb on your finger and take a leisurely walk on your hand. They are harmless and friendly to children. They do fly away, but if you move slowly and carefully around them, they will stay.

PRAYING MANTIS

A praying mantis is about as big as a garden bug gets, almost as long as a child's finger. They are a little hard to find as they change color to match the leaf on which they perch. Sometimes they are brown or green. The praying mantis is one of the original camouflage artists. Armies have copied their methods with spotted uniforms.

When these insects sit holding their arms together in front of them, they look like they are praying. That is how they got their unusual name. But it is really how they eat. They have voracious appetites and are indiscriminate eaters. Some days they are the gardener's friends and some days they are not. At times they go with the wrong crowd, eating friend and foe alike.

Their egg case looks a little like a wasps' nest with gray, crinkly-paperlike layers. The eggs hatch in the spring after a few weeks of warm weather.

A praying mantis changes its color to match the color of the plant on which it rests.

25

When the tiny creatures wiggle out between the thin flaps of their cases, they are very hard to see and the egg cases themselves lie undisturbed except for a tiny hole in the side.

APHIDS

The tiny aphid is hard to see. However, they travel with their families and a large family on a flower is easy to spot. Aphids are usually a soft green color, almost transparent. But they can be black or red. They are quick to multiply and they always stick with their ever-expanding family. At one week old, an aphid without a mate has a family, and as a family, they are very destructive. If five generations from one aphid were to live, more than 5 billion family members would exist.

Aphid families swarm on plants and literally suck the juices and life out of them. As they destroy plants, they secrete a liquid honeydew that ants love to eat. Ants are their good friends and follow them everywhere. If you see ants crawling on a plant, you know aphids have been there first. If a plant becomes overcrowded with aphids, they sprout wings and fly to another plant, and as they travel from plant to plant they also spread diseases.

Larry is examining and identifying an insect in his bug bottle before he releases it.

What aphids dread most is soapy water sprayed on them or a strong spray from the garden hose, an activity children love. Because of their small size, a whole family can quickly be washed off a plant. The soapy water also washes off the honeydew. Smart gardeners, at the first sign of an aphid, spray water on a plant every day for several days until they disappear.

GREEN LACEWING

An elegant, lovely lady, the frilly and fabulous green lacewing is a friend of all gardeners. Does your mother have a lacy hanky, blouse, or tablecloth? The patterns of the lacewing's lovely wings are often copied. But under those lacy wings is a very tough insect. Her nickname is the "aphid lion" because she eats so many aphids in such a short time. When green lacewings hatch from their eggs, they crawl up the nearest plants. When they reach the leaves, they eat for three weeks straight. They love to eat what gardeners hate, including aphids, spider mites, mealybugs and other assorted insects that attack plants. When they are stuffed full, they spin a white cocoon and sleep for a week. After they rest, they emerge as $3/4$-inch-long adults and lay eggs of their own, continuing the cycle.

Larry and Jake are looking for insects to collect in their bug bottles.

SPIDER MITES

Spider mites are as dirty, dangerous, devilish and disgusting as the aphids. They are quick and secretive devils, sometimes eating whole plants without being seen. A clan of spider mites speckles a plant with red dots like measles. If you think that spider mites have attacked your garden, hold a piece of white paper under the leaf, shake the plant, and a few will fall on the white paper. If you notice red specks, you have spider mites. You almost need a magnifying glass to see them.

Spider mites are not really spiders, in fact they are not even insects. They are closely related to the family of the horseshoe crab, although they have eight legs and spin webs. Imagine how quickly they can run with eight legs.

The spider mites suck moisture and chlorophyll from the leaves. Chlorophyll is what makes the leaves green and plants can't live without it as their leaves become yellow and wrinkled, die, and fall off.

TRICHOGRAMMA WASP

A Trichogramma wasp is completely harmless but frequently misjudged. Can you imagine being confused with misbehaving relatives? Imagine how hurt your feelings would be. The sad fact is the name "wasp" frightens most people. Even though they know nothing about the Trichogramma they often judge these wasps by their stinging relatives. The Trichogramma's young feed on the eggs of leafworms, fruitworms, cutworms, bullworms, and more than two hundred other species of pests. They are real friends to the gardener.

bugs through the mail

It has become a tradition in our home every spring to order bugs through the mail, both for the pleasure it gives the children, and the help it brings to our garden. We order ladybugs, praying mantis, Trichogramma wasps and green lacewings (all available from the Burpee catalogue) and each insect arrives differently. The ladybugs are our favorite. When they arrive, the race is on into the garden to

open the small box filled with straw and ladybugs. The kids pull out the straw and place it in different parts of the garden. A good deal of giggling among the kids ensues as they encourage the ladybugs to crawl on them. Our five-year-old considers them her special pets and gets excited whenever she sees them all summer long. One day I overheard her introducing her friend to "Lady," her pet ladybug.

The praying mantis arrive in small (3 to 4 inches) papery egg cases which you hang on shrubs or from the low branches of small trees. They hatch after experiencing two weeks of warm weather. When they emerge, the praying mantis are so tiny, crawling between the thin, papery flaps of their cases, that they leave little, if any, evidence of their emergence. If you are exceptionally lucky, and check during the hour or two it takes them to emerge, you might see the long-legged, elusive young, hanging on silken threads, drying out before they leap away, but perfect

timing is tricky. We have never seen them at this stage, even though each year we continue to check the cases to see if they have left. The way we know they have hatched after a spell of warm weather is to slice open the case and find it empty. When the praying mantis grow larger, they can be found in the garden.

Praying mantis nests are paperlike, gray egg cases.

Trichogramma wasp eggs are so small, 4,000 eggs can be attached to one square inch of cardboard.

If you want to see them when they hatch, put the egg case in a sealed paper bag near a radiator and the praying mantis will hatch in the bag. I was told they sound like popcorn popping as they hop around in the bag. A friend who kept her bag in the warm kitchen too long was chasing praying mantises out of the kitchen for days. So, unless you want them as house pets, remember to put the egg cases out in the garden as soon as they hatch.

When ordered through the mail, green lacewing eggs arrive mixed with rice hulls.

The Trichogramma wasps arrive with 4,000 teeny eggs attached to one square inch of cardboard, at the bottom of a paper cup. Look at them under a magnifying glass; or better yet, a microscope. Find a warm, humid place at the base of a plant in the garden to put the cup until the tiny, short-lived (8 to 10 days) adults emerge to parasitize as many as 100 pest eggs each.

The box of green lacewings' freshly-laid eggs arrives mixed with rice hulls. The kids shake and scatter the box contents around the base of plants. The green lacewings are tiny when they hatch, but instinctively crawl up plants, feeding for about three weeks on aphids, red spider mites, mealybugs, thrips and many different destructive insect eggs and larvae.

more of nature's creatures

Bats! To Get to Know Them Is to Love Them

Bats, the only mammal that can fly, eat up to 600 mosquitoes an hour, a feat we should applaud. They also pollinate and disperse the seeds of hundreds of trees and shrubs. Although a third of all mammals are bats, their population is declining faster than any other vertebrate in the world as people have chased them from their natural roosts.

Many untrue myths have developed about bats, and it is important to dispel the myths and to learn to respect and even welcome bats for the good they do. Of course they look scary as most are dark colored (black or brown) and fly with their mouths open to "echolocate" with delicate sonar that guides them through the darkness. They do not attack and will not fly into you. Bats can be found on summer evenings even in densely populated city parks.

Sy Montgomery, in her book, *Nature's Everyday Mysteries*, suggests a game that parents and children can play with bats by tossing a pebble up gently in front of a flying bat. The bat will sense it with its sonar and turn to fly towards it. The bat is smart enough to realize it is a stone and will not grab or eat it. This is a fascinating way to show your children how bats use sonar.

For more information on bats and how you can help save them, contact The Adirondack Nature Conservancy, P.O. Box 65, Keene Valley, NY 12943-9988.

Fireflies

Fireflies need no introduction to country children. They are always a pleasure to watch on summer evenings. Their tails glow off and on as if they were sending Morse code. Actually it is the female firefly sending a code to lure the males. Anyone with a flashlight can mimic their rhythm. Keep the flashlight pointed to the ground so the light isn't too bright, and if you flash with their rhythm, one second on, two seconds off, a firefly will approach and land on your hand.

Toads and Frogs

In early spring, if you live in the country, you may hear some strange noise coming from the garden. It is probably frogs, especially if your area is humid when they come out of hibernation. They gather in wet places on warm nights and sing their meeting and greeting song.

There are many species and many voices of frogs. Spotted leopard frogs emit throaty croaks while bullfrogs call jog-o-orum. The song of the green frog sounds like the twang of a loose banjo string but the frog in our garden sounds like a constant choking and chirping. All each wants is love.

Toads are similar in appearance to frogs but sing. They burrow into the soft garden soil living under plants. I have never known them to damage the plants and have on occasion dug a plant up and had a toad jump out at me. Both frogs and toads live on insects, so they are important for our gardens. They are also friendly and allow children to catch them.

Birds, Butterflies and Hummingbirds

With the loss of natural habitats, pushed back by the building boom of modern society, comes the loss of wild birds, bats, butterflies and hummingbirds as they are forced to move to new locations. To entice them to stay, a property has to provide appropriate nesting places, food and water. Water is the easiest to add by simply placing a birdbath or two in your yard. And children enjoy watching birds come to drink and bathe.

Nesting places are more complicated. The taller woody vines, with three or more branches emerging from a central stem, are a perfect nesting place for birds. Each spring, several nests of finches are found in the English ivy on the sides of our house. Blackbirds, robins, wrens and thrushes also look to nest in ivy. Last year birds' nests also appeared in two different climbing roses. Even on the porch, a hanging basket of vinca had a nest of baby finches.

If birds are nesting in your yard, they will feast on summer's bugs, a bonus for the gardener. Vines that bear fruit, especially berries that hang on the vine throughout the winter, such as Virginia creeper, rose hips, winter creeper and Boston ivy, provide food for birds throughout the difficult time of year. Your yard can become a year-round safe haven for many wild birds.

Summer brings hummingbirds to every part of the United States. They are fascinating to watch as they flit from bloom to bloom never stopping. Their wings beat about sixty times a second, making a humming sound. They do not have to land but can hover like a helicopter above the flowers and use their long beaks to drink the nectar. Often I hear them coming before I see them.

Red, especially, is irresistibly attractive to the hummingbird while orange or purple is scarcely less so. In a pinch, white might do. Red trumpet-shaped flowers are the hummingbird's first choice as only their long beaks are equipped to reach the nectar. The nectar, buried deep in the trumpet flowers, is safe from rival bees and butterflies.

It takes flowers planted in large conspicuous groups to attract the hummingbirds, but a single mature vine covered with flowers is conspicuous enough. This fact was reaffirmed when one morning, sitting in my bright red bathrobe drinking coffee on the back porch, a hummingbird boldly nose-dived at me. We were both startled and backed away, he, with wings flapping a hundred miles an hour, more dexterous than I.

A few favorite vines of hummingbirds are scarlet runner beans, nasturtiums, petunias, lilacs, morning glories, trumpet honeysuckle and obviously the hummingbird vine (*Asarina barclaiana*). Hummingbird feeders are also available from nurseries and garden stores. They are usually made of red plastic to be filled with sugar water (five parts water to one part sugar. The solution is boiled for a minute, then cooled before filling the feeder).

Butterfly kits make it easy to show a child the butterfly's life cycle.

While primarily nectar eaters, hummingbirds also snatch and eat large quantities of insects and spiders from the flowers they visit.

Butterflies also flock to nectar-rich blossoms and are equally attracted to bright colors and fragrance. They swarm to butterfly bushes like kids to a candystore. Pause if you can to watch them in their silent beauty as they flit from flower to flower, sipping nectar. They prefer a flat landing pad for a flower. The difficulty with butterflies is that, if you attract the adults, you must be respectful and also encourage babies, the "dreaded" caterpillars.

This brightly colored caterpillar is the larva of the swallowtail butterfly.

The passion vine is relishedby the caterpillars of the Fritillary butterfly (some varieties of Fritillary inhabit every part of North America). When its wings are spread, you can recognize the butterfly by its dull orange color decorated with black blotches. When the wings are closed, the underside is a checkerboard of silver with white or yellow spots edged in black.

The Monarch, probably the best loved of the butterflies, is also one of the showiest. Its brilliant orange wings are splattered with white dots and surrounded by black margins and veins. Butterflies are cold-blooded and need the sun's warmth to fly, so they are easier to see on cool days when they sit still and spread their wings to warm them. The caterpillars are white with black and yellow stripes, and birds know that they taste terrible because they eat the bitter milkweed sap.

Butterfly kits can be purchased from many children's educational stores, including The Nature Company. The kits contain a butterfly tent and a coupon to send for small caterpillars. Within a few days of their arrival, the caterpillars will spin a silk cocoon and go into their chrysalis stage. In another seven to ten days they emerge as butterflies to stretch their wings.

To attract butterflies to the garden, provide them with the type of plants they like. The butterfly bush (*Buddleia*) is the most obvious and the easiest to grow. It is also fragrant and beautiful with long spikes of white, pink, blue or purple flowers blooming from mid to late summer. The Connecticut Audubon Society recommends perennials for attracting butterflies, including bee balm, cardinal flower, sweet William, liatris, coneflower and shasta daisy. Always remember that butterflies at different stages of their development need different types of plants.

The butterfly lays her eggs on a plant that will provide food for the hungry, slow-moving caterpillar stage. Caterpillars can do quite a lot of damage to a plant but if you want the butterflies, you have to respect the caterpillars. If you learn to recognize the caterpillars, you have the option of moving them from a plant you cherish to another that you prefer they eat. Many butterfly lovers grow a row of parsley especially for caterpillars. When a caterpillar is found, it can be picked up and moved to its own parsley plant. One plant supports one caterpillar.

Because caterpillars move so slowly and are so easily caught, they have their own defensive mechanisms. Some caterpillars look like a leaf, a stem, or even a bird dropping so they are not readily seen by their enemies, mostly birds. Some look like scary monsters with bright spots painted to look like eyes, while others are decorated with false faces to resemble tiny snakes. A few caterpillars have bodies covered with sharp spines or contain indigestible poisons. All in all, they are a fascinating family for you and your children to get to know better.

Moths

Another interesting attraction in the three-ring circus summer garden is the nighttime activity of the moth, the Japanese honeysuckle and the moonflower. Both vines open their flowers at night, pure white and especially fragrant, to attract night-flying moths. The moonflowers die at dusk while the fertilized honeysuckle flowers change colors from white to yellow. Both white and yellow flowers are present and long-lasting on the honeysuckle vine.

What could be a more beautiful
playground for children
than a flower garden?

2

gardens designed for kids

garden designs

Think of a garden as an outdoor playroom—a place to encourage children's imagination, surrounded by nature's bounty. Do not worry if it looks messy at times. It is more important to celebrate and observe the growth of plants and to enjoy getting your hands dirty. It does not matter if you have never gardened before. Gardening is an active sport best learned by trial and error. If you are observant, the garden will teach you more than books could ever tell.

Every gardener at one time or another has mistakenly pulled a plant thinking it was a weed and let a weed grow thinking it was a plant. This will happen to you too. Do not worry about the particulars. As long as you prepare the soil properly and remember to water the garden regularly, you will have success.

Remember, a garden is a world of limitless imagination, a place for reflection amid calm beauty where you can closely observe nature as your garden endlessly unfolds its beauty. Flowers, depending on their personality and character, give of themselves and often become lifelong friends. Even the most mundane of garden chores brings you close to the ever-changing seasons as never before you witness the beauty in the passing storms, the coming and going of perennials and the cooling of light rains as they bathe and cleanse the earth.

Mother Nature is the irrepressible optimist and her optimism rubs off on the gardener. In the garden she entertains us with the songs of birds, the dances of butterflies and hummingbirds and the gymnastics of toads and praying mantises.

Each day you spend close to nature, you will make new discoveries. A garden is constantly changing as its productivity is influenced by the twists of nature. The temperature, rainfall, nutrients in the soil and the population of local insects all play a part. The elements combine to make gardening interesting and exciting. With so many variables, each summer in the garden is different. Even if you grow the same plants and repeat favorite activities from year to year, you will never have exactly the same results. The children, as they age and grow more comfortable in the garden, will put their own twist on the garden activities and crafts. Of course it has all been done before but never quite the same way, just as the same recipe prepared by different people will yield a variety of results. Even to an experienced gardener, a lifetime is too short to learn all that the garden has to teach.

These garden designs are for young people of all ages—and that includes the young at heart. Hopefully, children, parents and grandparents will find it joyful and practical. Each garden is planned to bring out the best in children and to help their imagination grow.

All the gardens in this chapter are appropriate for children of any age. However, the younger the child, the more responsibility falls to the parents.

In the most successful children's gardens, the work is shared between adult and child—with the adult doing most of the work. If you already grow a vegetable garden, small children can help with the planting, the watering and the harvesting. They are not usually interested in weeding.

Older kids may be given a corner of the garden for their own use where they can dig without hurting the plants of others. When my youngest daughter, Catie, decided she wanted her own garden, we gave her a corner of the vegetable garden. She selected flowering annuals from a nursery. I helped her to arrange them in her garden by color and height only to find she dug them up and moved them around three more times that week. The plants didn't do very well, but Catie had a wonderful time and that's what counts in a child's first garden.

tepee garden

Seed List

A. Scarlet runner bean

B. Jack-be-little pumpkin

C. Radish mix

D. Mammoth sunflower

E. Marigolds

F. Strawflowers

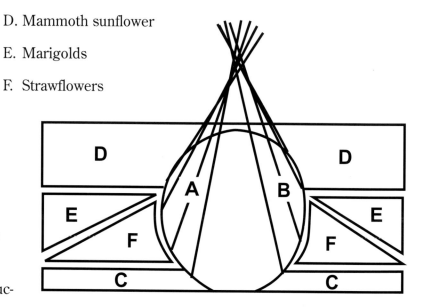

A vine-covered tepee is easy to grow. Young children delight in watching the vines climb up the tepee poles, creating a special place for them to hide and play. I recommend two fast-growing vines. The most important one is the scarlet runner bean which, alone, quickly covers the structure. The vine is continuously covered with both red flowers and beans all summer. It offers children the best of both worlds: being able to hide in the tepee and to reach out and grab a young pod to nibble. The second vine, Jack-be-little pumpkin, will not cover the tepee, but grows pumpkins so small that they fit in children's hands. Other fast-growing vines that could be substituted are morning glory, moonflower and love-in-a-puff.

At the backside of the tepee, stately sunflowers are planted to "stand guard" over the garden and grow seeds that children can harvest for bird feed or roast for snacks. In the front and side of the garden, marigolds grow to be picked for fresh flower bouquets and strawflowers for dried winter bouquets (see pages 68–70).

Prepare the garden soil for tepees as you would for any new garden (see page 7). After the danger of spring frost, sow the seeds directly in the garden where they are to grow, following the instructions on each seed package. I positioned the tepee in the middle of the garden, but you can place it anywhere and adjust the design accordingly. The tepee itself was made of bamboo poles set in the ground and tied together at the top. A trellis netting can be wrapped around the poles to make it easier for the vines to climb and cover the tepee structure. The scarlet runner beans and the Jack-be-little pumpkin seeds should both be planted evenly spaced, a few inches apart, around the outside tepee structure. When the seedlings emerge, they can be thinned to the distance recommended on the seed packets. A large plastic garbage bag can be laid on the ground inside the tepee to keep weeds from growing. Later when the vines are covering the tepee and the children want to play inside it, a towel or a small rug can be laid for the children. Radishes quickly mature and can be eaten in three to four weeks.

Catie Dales hides from the sun in the shade of her tepee garden.

43

kids' korner

Seed List
(Other varieties can easily be substituted)

A. Nasturtium 'Alaska'

B. Marigold 'Lemon Gem'

C. Carrots 'Little Finger'

D. Sunflower 'Sunspot'

E. Beans, purple pod 'Royal Burgundy'

F. Cosmos 'Bright Lights'

G. Small fancy gourds, mixed

Each seed was selected to teach children something different about the fun of gardening:

The small and fancy gourds fascinate children because of their variety of shapes, colors and texture. They can be shaped like an apple, orange, pear, egg or bottle. Some are striped, others spotted and a few plain. Their skin can be smooth or covered in worts like the back of a toad.

Both the gourds and beans are grown to climb a corner fence.

The sunflower has enormous flowers, 12 inches across on 18-inch stems.

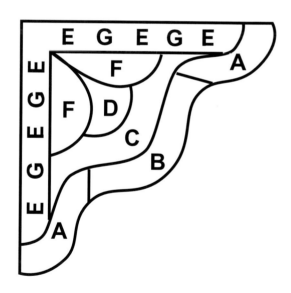

The taller, 3-foot-high Mexican sunflower and 4-foot-high cosmos are beautiful in the garden and plentiful for bouquets. Both flowers attract butterflies.

Nasturtiums, with their variegated leaf patterns, edible flowers and quick bloom teach an important lesson.

Carrots 'Little Finger' is a name the children will remember and understand. They are ready to be picked in 62 days and can be eaten straight from the garden.

'Royal Burgundy' beans change like magic, from purple to dark green, when dropped in boiling water.

Marigold 'Lemon Gem' has fine, lacy foliage that is lemon scented. The flowers also taste like lemon and can be used in salads or dried and cooked in muffins.

butterfly and hummingbird garden

Seed List

A. Nasturtium

B. Zinnias

C. Celosia

D. Nicotiana

E. Cosmos

F. Mexican sunflower

Butterflies and hummingbirds are fascinating to watch as they flit around the garden. Although both exist throughout North America, they will not visit a garden unless it has flowers that attract them (see pages 33–36). To encourage them to come and to stay, grow bright

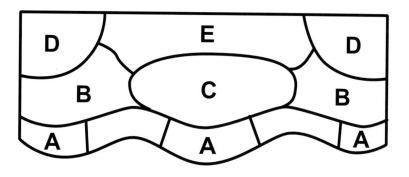

red, trumpet-shaped, fragrant flowers for hummingbirds and brightly colored, flat flowers, a favorite landing pad, for butterflies. These flowers will bloom until hard frost, and you will get a generous bonus of flowers to cut for bouquets.

This garden is easy to grow from seed sown directly in the prepared soil after the danger of frost has passed. Follow the planting directions on each seed packet and water with a fine spray to keep the seeds from washing away. Covering the garden with a lawn and garden blanket for 3 to 4 weeks will create a favorable environment, fostering better seed and faster, stronger growth. Keep the soil evenly moist until the seedlings emerge (7 to 21 days, depending on the variety of seed, soil and weather conditions) and are well established. When the seedlings are 2 inches high, thin them so the plants are spaced 8 inches apart for nasturtiums, 12 inches apart for zinnias, celosia, nicotiana and cosmos, and 24 inches apart for Mexican sunflowers. You can use the thinnings to fill in any gaps in your garden plantings or you can grow them in pots.

Be sure to keep your spent flowers picked as this prolongs and increases flower production. This garden grows enough flowers to attract hummingbirds and butterflies and to cut for bouquets. Celosia, cosmos, Mexican sunflower and zinnia are all excellent cut flowers. Celosia is also fine for dried arrangements.

a sunflower house

A sunflower house is a magical place for children to play. The house can be grown in different sizes; the one pictured is a rectangle, 4 feet wide and 8 feet long, made by a dozen and a half sunflowers each spaced 1 foot apart, leaving a two foot opening on one side for a door. This size allows a children's table and chairs to be placed inside for tea parties. It could, however, be smaller to accommodate a blanket or beach towel on the ground for children to sit.

The most charming sunflower houses are topped with a roof of morning glories, but achieving this is a little tricky. The sunflowers and the morning glories should be planted at the same time, after the last frost. Plant

Sunflowers grow fast to tower over children. A sunflower house will give them many hours of play in the garden.

morning glories outside of the rectangle of sunflowers. Plant extra sunflowers and morning glories, then weed out the excess when they reach a few inches in height.

The sunflowers will show themselves first. As the morning glories grow, they will twine clockwise around and up the sunflowers. It is important to remember clockwise direction when training the morning glories at the beginning of their ascent. If you twist them counter-clockwise, they will slowly unwind and rewrap themselves clockwise. When the sunflowers are four feet high, tie string under their heads and stretch it from one sunflower to another directly across from it, then back again to its neighbor simulating "a cat's cradle." The string provides the morning glories a roof framework to grow along.

The sunflower house can be decorated many different ways. Stuffed animals can be tied to the sunflowers as if they were climbing up their stalks. But you will see that your children's imagination will find their own unique directions.

gardens-on-the-go

Flowerpots come in all sizes and shapes, but pots are not the only appropriate containers. Almost anything that will hold soil can be used as a "flowerpot." Old shoes, coffee cans, baby carriages, wheelbarrows, wagons and buckets work quite well.

It is not important what the container is, but whether it is clean, able to hold soil and water, and easy for kids to move from place to place as the spirit catches them. Containers without drainage holes can be used, but good results are more difficult since more plants die from drowning than from thirst.

Let your imagination loose. On a trip to the beach for example, let the children collect sea shells as pots for small plants. Baby's tears, tiny African violets or small succulents can live indoors for many years in a conch shell.

Plant grass seed in a child's old shoes or outgrown rubber boot. It will grow fast and can be trimmed into designs with scissors for fun. Even an old toy could become a planter; wooden wagons, plastic sand pails or a set of play dishes also work well. Containers recycled from the kitchen, such as milk or egg cartons and soup cans, are also used for starting seeds.

A moveable garden can be planted in a wheelbarrow.

Wagons or wheelbarrows (anything on wheels) make especially wonderful planters for children. What could be better than a garden they can wheel around to show visitors? It is also practical as it can be moved to give the plants more sun or shade, or to protect them from foul weather. Beware, however: As the kids move it around, you might have to go looking for it each time it needs water.

Public Children's Gardens Around the Country

There are many public children's gardens around the country, and visiting them with your children can be enjoyable as well as inspirational and educational.

MICHIGAN STATE UNIVERSITY 4H CHILDREN'S GARDEN

Those who live in Michigan, my home state, are lucky to be close to Jane Taylor's exceptional children's garden opened in 1992 at Michigan State University. It is the most innovative and creative in the country.

When you visit, plan to spend many hours to allow the children to browse and play as they enjoy the different gardens.

Disney World's children's garden is a wonderful and creative place to take a child of any age.

The American Horticultural Society's garden in Alexandria, Virginia, introduces children to the fun of gardening.

continues on page 52

51

continued from page 51

First, climb up the wooden tree post for an overall view of the ninety theme gardens. Here are a few of my favorites:

Walk through a maze of green foliage and see sculptures of a grinning Cheshire Cat, the Queen of Hearts and the White Rabbit complete with pocket watch. Alice would have felt right at home.

A pizza garden is shaped and divided like a six-slice pizza. Each slice is planted with a different ingredient: tomatoes, peppers, onions, thyme, basil and oregano.

An alphabet garden, with each letter in the alphabet represented by a plant whose name begins with the appropriate letter: A is for aster, B is for begonia, C is for cosmos and on through the alphabet.

In the cereal bowl garden corn, rice, rye and oats are grown.

Jack and the Giant's garden is planted with sunflowers, giant cabbages, and a beanstalk.

A butterfly garden, shaped like a butterfly and planted with flowers, attracts butterflies of all colors.

Throughout the garden are signs that read "Please touch gently," and "Never do not touch." It is a garden to please all the senses. Even if you can not visit, feel free to borrow some of their garden ideas for your own.

There are many children's gardens scattered across America. Check to see which are close to your home. Following is the American Horticultural Society's List of Children's Gardening Programs at Public Gardens and Horticultural Societies.

Mid-Atlantic

The American Horticultural Society River Farm
7931 East Boulevard Drive
Alexandria, VA 22308-1300

Brookside Gardens
1500 Glenallan Avenue
Wheaton, MD 20902

Frelinghuysen Arboretum
P.O. Box 1295
Morristown, NJ 07962-1295

Green Springs Garden Park
4603 Green Spring Road
Alexandria, VA 22312

Longwood Gardens
Box 501
Kennett Square, PA 19348-0501

Morris Arboretum of the University of Pennsylvania
9414 Meadowbrook Avenue
Philadelphia, PA 19118

Norfolk Botanical Garden
Azalea Garden Road
Norfolk, VA 23518

Tudor Place Foundation, Inc.
1605 32nd Street N.W.
Washington, DC 20007

continues on page 54

continued from page 53

**The Tyler Arboretum Field
and Forest Comparison**
515 Painter Road
Media, PA 19063-4424

**U.S. National Arboretum USDA,
Agricultural Research Service**
3501 New York Avenue N.E.
Washington, DC 20002

Midwest

**Chicago Botanic Garden Longitudinal
Plant ScienceCurriculum**
P.O. Box 400
Glencoe, IL 60022

Garden Center of Greater Cleveland
11030 East Boulevard
Cleveland, OH 44106

Green Bay Botanical Garden
P.O. Box 1913
Green Bay, WI 54305-1913

**Michigan State University 4-H
Children's Garden**
4700 Sough Hagadorn Road, Suite 220
Hannah Technology and Research Center
East Lansing, MI 48823-5399

Minnesota Landscape Arboretum
3675 Arboretum Drive
P.O. Box 39
Chanhassen, MN 55317

Missouri Botanical Garden
4344 Shaw Boulevard
St. Louis, MO 63110

Northeast

Brooklyn Botanic Garden
1000 Washington Avenue
Brooklyn, NY 11225-1099

Massachusetts Horticultural Society
Horticultural Hall
300 Massachusetts Avenue
Boston, MA 02115

New York Botanical Garden
200th and Southern Boulevard
Bronx, New York, 10458-5126
718-817-8700

South

Dallas Arboretum and Botanic Garden
8617 Garland Road
Dallas, TX 75218

Southeast

Atlantic Botanical Garden
Piedmont Park at the Prado
Box 77246
Atlanta, GA 30357

Box Tower Garden
P.O. Box 3810
Lake Wales, FL 33859-3810

Callaway Gardens
Pine Mountain, GA 31822

North Carolina State University Arboretum
Department of Horticultural Science
Box 7609
Raleigh, NC 27695-7609

**Reynolda Gardens of
  Wake Forest University**
100 Reynolda Village
Winston-Salem, NC 27106

Walt Disney World
Seminar Productions
P.O. Box 40
Lake Buena Vista, FL 32830

Southwest

Desert Botanical Garden
1201 North Galvin Parkway
Phoenix, AZ 85008

West

Disneyland Park
1313 South Harbor Boulevard
Anaheim, CA 92802

Santa Barbara Botanic Garden
1212 Mission Canyon Road
Santa Barbara, CA 93105

National Tropical Botanic Garden
Hawaii Plant Conservation Center
P.O. Box 340
Lawai, Kauai, HI 96765

Strybing Arboretum and Botanical Gardens
Golden Gate Park
Ninth Avenue at Lincoln Way
San Francisco, CA 94122

Canada

Royal Botanical Gardens
Box 399
Hamilton, ON L8N 3H8
University of British Columbia

The Botanical Garden
6501 N.W. Marine Drive
Vancouver, BC V6T 1W5

University of Guelph Arboretum
Guelph, ON N1G 2W1

Flowers can be strung
with a needle and thread to
make necklaces and wreaths
for dolls or stuffed animals.

3

kids' crafts
and activities

scarecrows

While scarecrows don't keep birds and animals out of the garden, they do add humor and fun. Visitors can't help smiling at their appearance.

Making a scarecrow is a creative project for the whole family. The traditional approach is to start with two strong poles or boards (two broomsticks are perfect). One should be 5 to 6 feet long, the other 2 to 3 feet long. Nail or tie together the wood with heavy twine in the shape of a cross. Then

The making of a scarecrow encourages imagination in children and parents alike. Pictured here are ideas to get you started.

pound the longer pole into the ground deep enough to support the cross.

Dressing the scarecrow to give it personality is the most fun. The head can be made from a pillowcase or a nylon stocking stuffed with hay or straw. The eyes, mouth and nose can be drawn with permanent markers, then a rag mop or yarn for hair, topped with a baseball cap or straw hat, completes the ensemble. The head is slipped over the pole and tied just above the vertical pole to form the neck. Next, a shirt and pants are added, each stuffed and fitted around the pole. For hands, gloves can be pinned to the shirt sleeves. Extra features such as a rake, a scarf or a sign can be added.

Over the summer, this lady scarecrow grew a dress of flowering vines.

There are many variations on this basic structure. For example, the poles can be dressed without stuffing or can be made to look like an animal or a space monster instead of a human.

One year our lady scarecrow had a flowering-vine dress. The scarecrow "T" structure was a trellis, a stuffed head was placed on top and clear fishing line was strung from her armpits to the ground for the vines to climb. By midsummer, our lady had a flowering skirt and by summer's end the skirt had grown into a dress. We used scarlet runner beans, but any fast-growing vines will do.

"The Little Woman": A Chicken Wire Sculpture

We made "the little woman" one summer. Her floor-length skirt was a cylinder of chicken wire with a diameter of 16 inches, cinched at the waist. A second, smaller piece of chicken wire, with a diameter of 8 inches, was attached on top and squished into the shape of a bodice. The arms and head were separate pieces of chicken wire attached to the body, and the ends of the wires were twisted together to hold its shape. Clinging annual vines can be grown over chicken wire sculptured into the shape of a person, an animal or an object. Chicken wire can be cut, rolled and squeezed into any shape, but the simpler the figure, the easier it is to cover.

A "Little Woman" garden sculpture was molded from chicken wire and planted with vines.

We filled the empty chicken wire sculpture with potting soil so some of the flowers and vines could be grown out of it, but it could easily be left empty. To stabilize larger sculptures, broomstick-size poles can be tied together at the top, tepee fashion, and pushed into the soil within the chicken wire. The climbing snapdragon (*Asarina*) is one of the best annual vines for clinging, forming an even mat of green as it climbs. Other vines such as nasturtium, morning glory and scarlet runner bean do well, but they have to be pruned to hold their shape.

Pot Lady

If you have been gardening for a long time and have terra-cotta or plastic pots to spare, a "pot lady" can add a new, distinct personality to your garden. The pot lady can be any size depending on the pots used.

"Pot Lady" is made from terra-cotta pots strung together. She wears an apron and a hat as she jauntily sits on the garden bench.

To make a pot lady as shown in the picture, nine small pots are needed for each leg and six for each arm (thirty small pots in all). In addition, two large pots are needed for the body, a medium-size pot for the head and a small one for the neck. The pot lady can be seated on the ground, placed on a bench or propped up to stand tall.

Make the body first, stacking two large pots on top of each other; the bottom pot should be right side up and the second pot should be upside down. They meet to form the waist. The head can be made two different ways: I use a small pot for the neck and a medium size pot for the head, which is filled with potting soil and planted with parsley for hair. If you prefer not to have something growing, a head can be made by stacking two pots a few sizes smaller than the body, in the same way, on top of the larger pot. The arms and legs are made with smaller pots stacked inside each other. A rope is threaded through the holes in the bottom of the pots linking them loosely together between the rim of one pot and the base of another. Moss is stuffed in

61

the bottom of the pots to help hold them apart and to allow "knees" and "elbows" to bend. The rope can be tied to the end pot (where the head goes), and then the other end is looped and tied around the neck. Clothes, aprons, hats, gloves and T-shirts are optional.

Monster Greeters

Getting help from children to rake leaves is always a struggle. However, in late October you may catch their attention with the coming of Halloween. Harvest or buy a pumpkin approximately the size of your head. Children love to help create a "scary monster" to decorate the porch for Halloween, and this is also an ideal way to get the kids to rake up the leaves.

Grab your old clothes, the ones that should have been thrown away a long time ago. Stuff the clothes with Fall leaves to make the shape of a bulky person. Arrange the pants on a step or a chair with a back as if the monster were sitting and balance the shirt on top. A yardstick or tree branch, poked through the shirt and into the pants, will help hold them together so your monster sits upright.

Now comes the tricky part—holding the pumpkin on the shoulders. If the pumpkin is carved, it can be balanced on the stick and perhaps tied to the back of

A "Monster Greeter" is made from old clothes stuffed with fallen leaves. He is ready to greet the Halloween trick-or-treaters.

the chair. If it is too heavy, a box or small log can be placed on end, inside the shirt, to hold it or the monster can simply hold his head in his lap.

Another alternative to a heavy pumpkin can be a stuffed monster mask added as the head. Your monster can be outfitted with scarves, ties, hats, jewelry, boots or anything else the kids dream up. They'll probable giggle and squirm as they consider what to have him hold (green and red cooked fettuccine noodles remind the children of innards, but if you're faint of heart, a flashlight will do). Be sure to let the kids name him.

If there are more leaves to rake or a large pile left over, it can be a great treat to let the children run and jump in them. Don't pile them too high or the younger kids might disappear under the leaves. It won't hurt them, but it can be scary. The good news about the children jumping in the leaves is that they will be smashing them into smaller pieces, and they will compost faster. If the pile is jumped in enough, the leaves can be returned directly to the garden. The bad news is you'll have to rake the leaves into a pile again and this time the kids will certainly disappear.

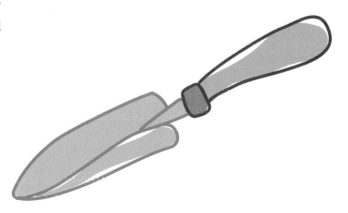

A sense of humor grows in a garden when funny planters such as this frog stand guard.

63

for the fun of it, try the unexpected

Alittle laughter with the kids is a healthy thing. It's fun to be silly doing the unexpected, such as decorating a straw hat with vegetables, Chinese lanterns, peas or peppers. For the less outrageous, decorating a wreath with vegetables will do.

Vegetables such as pumpkins, gourds and cabbages make funny vases for flowers.

Dishes shaped like a vegetable are a popular motif today, but it can be more fun to use the vegetables themselves as dishes. Many vegetables, when hollowed out, can be used as vases for flowers (eggplant, acorn squash, peppers), or even a serving bowl for soup as in the case of pumpkins or other rounded squash. A large pumpkin with the top removed and the seeds scooped out makes an interesting soup tureen. At Halloween, I have filled it with chili for a children's party and, for Thanksgiving, a squash soup.

Cabbages hold small amounts of water in the spaces between the leaves and flowers can easily be tucked into them. After the

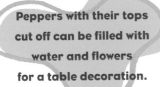
A cabbage can hold water between its leaves. In this picture, roses are tucked in between the leaves for a blooming present for grandmother.

flowers in the arrangement fade, the cabbage can still be eaten. Melons, gourds, and even peppers can be used as unique candleholders or vases, sometimes carved with designs as traditional as pumpkins at Halloween, or used as a base for long, tapered candles.

Peppers with their tops cut off can be filled with water and flowers for a table decoration.

65

too much zucchini

My six zucchini plants more than feed my family of seven, weekend guests and neighbors all summer. After exhaustedly boiling, sautéing, baking tiny zucchini, and puréeing larger ones into bread and soup, we still are always surprised to find several hiding, in spite of their baseball-bat size, under even larger leaves. There is no getting around it, zucchinis are prolific. Conventional wisdom in peaceful Vermont advises locking cars at shopping centers in August to avoid returning to find your car filled with zucchini left by an overproductive gardener.

One playful solution to an abundance of zucchini is to turn the largest zucchini into a peacock. To duplicate my peacock you will need:

A zucchini the size of a baseball bat can be turned into a peacock complete with a flowering tail.

one baseball-bat-size zucchini

assorted long-stem flowers

several fern leaves

2 peppers

a brick of floral foam

floral tape

a knife

a spoon

small-leafed ivy

cockscomb (celosia)

Queen Anne's lace

If you do not have the flowers I used, substitute your own or florist's flowers for an original variation.

Place the zucchini on an oval platter and position it so that the neck points upward. Slice $1/4$ inch or so off the bottom, to allow it to sit flat. Next scoop out an oval near the back of the zucchini for your peacock's tail. Remove all the seeds (the zucchini you scoop out can be used for making bread or soup). Cut a section of floral foam to fill the hole. Soak the shaped floral foam in warm water for half an hour. When placed in the opening, the floral foam will add weight and help balance the flower arrangement. While the floral foam is soaking, pick your flowers. The best flowers to use have arching shapes that will form a graceful tail that can be viewed from all sides. If it is to be viewed from three sides, arrange them straight in a fan of a strutting peacock. Look for round, brightly colored flowers to fashion the "eyes" of a circle design found in the tail of a real peacock.

Fill the hole in the zucchini with the soaked floral foam. The head, beak and comb can be fashioned from lightweight, colorful peppers and attached with straight pins. Slice an opening for the beak. As the pepper dries over the next few hours, the beak will open. A flower can even be inserted in the mouth. Use a layer of ferns to shape the wings and tail feathers. Small-leafed ivy can form a collar where the neck and body meet and where the head meets the neck. You can add a frilled collar with Queen Anne's lace around the neck. The peacock may be a little quirky, but it contains the seeds of a smile and amuses children and guests.

everlasting flowers

Winter, with all its holidays, can be made brighter with the colorful flowers of everlastings. Everlastings are flowers that dry naturally and are preserved in their true flower shape and color. Some everlastings, strawflowers and globe amaranth, for example, have papery petals that look the same whether they are fresh or dry. Their color will stay bright throughout the winter and beyond if they are not faded by the sun.

The best way to save everlasting flowers for fall and winter bouquets is to cut them just before the peak of bloom in fall. The longer you leave them out after they bloom, the more likely rain or wind will damage their perfection. Flowers for drying should be cut in the heat of the day. (Rather than conserving moisture, as with cut flowers, with everlastings you squander it.) Strip off the leaves, and hang the flowers upside down in small bunches, held together by rubber bands, in a dark, warm, dry place. As the flowers dry and shrink, the band will continue to hold the flowers and the weight of the flowers will pull the stem straight while they dry and stiffen. Once dried, they'll last until fresh flower time next spring.

Rachel is collecting everlasting flowers to make into bouquets for Christmas presents.

An assortment of dried flowers hangs upside down to straighten their stems before they are arranged in vases.

If you are close to the sea and have very humid summers, hang the flowers in a small closet with a dehumidifier. Without it, the flowers will mildew and rot, rather than dry.

Flowers for air-drying include:

Ageratum	Goldenrod
Artemisia	Joe-pye weed
Astilbe	Lavender
Baby's breath	Sedum 'Autumn Joy'
Bells of Ireland	Statice
Blue salvia	Strawflowers
Calendula	Winged everlasting
Celosia	Xeranthemum
Dusty miller	Yarrow
Echinops	

Some flowers have sculptural seedpods that dry naturally and hold their shape and color through the winter. You and the kids can collect these wild plants and seeds from fields and roadsides. They can make a simple, yet elegant fall decoration when placed in a bowl on a table or in a box next to a fireplace. Look around your area and you'll find many more. The popular ones are:

Acorns	Pinecones
Chinese lanterns	Poppy
Money Plant	Black-eyed Susan
Milkweed	Thistles

Older kids can use a variety of seedpods, pinecones and dried flowers to decorate a basket. The pinecones can be wired to the basket while the smaller seedpods and dried flowers are glued (Elmer's glue or a quick-drying cement works well).

Dried flowers and seedpods are fragile and should be handled carefully if they are to be used in dried bouquets. The stems are often weak and break off while drying. Green floral wire or floral picks with wire attached can be wound around the stem for strength or can replace the stem entirely.

Dry floral foam or Styrofoam can be used as a base for arranging bouquets of dried flowers. Styrofoam comes in a variety of shapes and can be used for making any number of dried-flower arrangements, from Christmas trees to topiaries. Use a pencil or other pointed object to make a hole in the Styrofoam. Squeeze a drop of quick-drying cement in the hole and push the flower gently into place. After your arrangement is complete, spray with an unscented hair spray to hold your fragile flower petals in place.

To dust a longer-lived arrangement, use a hair dryer on a low setting to gently blow off the dust.

cut flowers

Picking bouquets of flowers from the garden as gifts to share with friends, grandparents and parents is an activity that is simple for children of all ages.

One summer, my daughter and her cousin decided they needed more spending money so they set up a flower stand instead of the more traditional lemonade stand. They had a good time while filling their pockets with change.

If you teach your kids the proper way to treat freshly cut flowers, you will be rewarded with longer-lasting bouquets. The time of day to gather cut flowers is when the sun is low, in the morning or evening. Stems are apt to wilt quickly if cut in midday when the sun is hot and the plant is losing water. If you must cut in the middle of the day, carry a clean bucket (not metal to which some flowers react) of warm water and immerse the stems directly after they are cut.

Cut flowers arranged in recycled cans and bottles are an easy way to give presents from the garden.

Most flowers are ready to cut when the buds are about half open. If the buds are in a small cluster, cut them when they first open, including some unopened buds, which will become healthy blooms lengthening the lifetime of the bouquet.

A few flowers, including zinnias, marigolds, asters and dahlias, should be picked in full bloom, as these will last and continue to bloom well in their new surroundings.

Cut the flower stems on an angle to allow a larger surface to absorb water. Cut each stem as long as possible without taking too many upopened buds. Longer stem-lengths give you more options when arranging. Make the cut with clean, sharp scissors as you do not want to crush or bruise the stems.

Grow a "garbage garden" from the tops of root vegetables.

Remove leaves at the bottom of the stem; leaves left on the stem underwater decay and smell unpleasant. If you have cut the flowers in the garden and not put them directly into water, recut the stems after you bring them inside, before conditioning them. The bottom of the stems begin to dry if left out of water for even a few minutes.

The most effective steps for prolonging the blooming of your cut flowers are those taken early. You want the plants to absorb as much water as possible, and you can sometimes double the life of the cut flowers by plunging them in warm water as soon as possible after picking. Some experts recommend the temperature of the water be the same as the air to minimize the shock of being cut. Remember, the emphasis is on warm water, though it's easy to think the opposite. You splash your face with cold water to stimulate and wake up your senses, but with flowers the opposite holds. Warmth stimulates, but cold slows down the life within plants.

After cutting and immersing the flowers in warm water, place them in a cool place for 4 to 12 hours to allow the stems to completely fill with water. The cool air and warm water combination conditions the flowers and extends their life away from the garden.

Add a few drops of liquid household bleach and a teaspoon of sugar to the water. The bleach will do what it does for swimming pools—prevent fungus from growing (it will not harm the blossoms). The sugar will be quick-energy food, but if used without the bleach, it will speed the growth of fungus.

arranging flowers

Abby and Catie had a summer business of selling cut flowers to passing cars.

Your kids' flower arrangements need not be elaborate and time-consuming. Float a single flower in a bowl, put an individual, long-stemmed flower in a slim, tall vase, or cut the stems short and place flowers individually in a series of miniature glass bottles and group them together on a table. Try a tightly packed arrangement of one type of flower, emphasizing the flower, not the container. Sometimes an arrangement is even more effective if the leaves are stripped off and the focus is only on the flowers.

73

Flowers for Dinner

Flowers have been considered food by many cultures for centuries. The Japanese cook daylily buds, the Italians fry zucchini blossoms and the French make rose-flavored deserts. Always check whether a flower is edible before tasting it, and never eat flowers sprayed with chemicals or flowers bought from the florist. Flowers can be used in a multitude of ways: to add color and taste to salads; to decorate a pad of butter; to float in drinks, or to use as garnishes. Some flowers, like tulips and zucchini blossoms, are large enough to stuff with chicken or other main course salads.

CAUTION: Some flowers are poisonous: potato, foxgloves and sweet pea, to name a few. Make sure you know the difference.

Before cooking with a flower, taste it to see if you like its flavor. Flowers with strong scents like lavender may be overpowering and should be used sparingly.

There are hundreds of varieties of marigolds that are very spicy and taste awful. It is important to taste the flowers before you cook with them. Rosalind Creasy, an American expert on edible flowers, suffered through many unpleasant varieties to find the best and she recommends the Climax series, 'Lemon Gem', and 'White Snowbird' marigolds. Marigold petals dry easily and can be stored in an airtight jar for winter use in cakes, breads and muffins. The flowers in the list above are edible.

COMMON NAME	LATIN NAME
Bee Balm	*Monarda* species
Cornflowers	*Centaurea cyanus*
Day lilies	*Hemerocallis* species
Pinks	*Dianthus* species
Hollyhocks	*Alcea rosea*
Honeysuckle	*Loniecera japonica*
Jasmine	*Jasminum* species
Johnny-jump-ups	*Viola x wittrockiana*
Lilacs	*Syringa vulgaris*
Marigolds	*Tagetes* species
Nasturtiums	*Tropaeolum* species
Pansy	*Viola x wittrockiana*
Roses	*Rosa* species
Scented geraniums	*Pelargonium* species
Tuberous begonia	*Begonia x tuberhybrida*
Tulip	*Tulipa* species
Violets	*Viola cornuta*

Edible flowers from vegetables and fruits

apple blossoms

broccoli flowers

pea blossoms (*not* sweetpea blossoms, which are poisonous)

plum blossoms

scarlet runner bean blossoms

strawberry blossoms

squash and zucchini blossoms

candied flowers

Many flowers can be candy coated for tasty treats or used as decoration for desserts. This practice was common in seventeenth- and eighteenth-century Europe and is so simple children can do it. The flowers that work best are violets, Johnny-jump-ups, scented geraniums, pansies and rose petals. All that is needed is a gently beaten egg white, a small paintbrush and very fine sugar.

Edible flowers can be preserved as a hard candy by painting them with egg whites and then sprinkling them with sugar.

Wash the flowers gently in cool running water, pat them dry, paint with egg white on both sides and sprinkle with fine sugar. The flowers must be completely covered with egg white and sugar which act as a preservative. The color and shape will last for months or even a year if stored in a dry place away from sunlight which fades them. Allow them to dry and harden on a colander or on a clean screen where there is good air circulation and low humidity. When dry, the blossoms will be hard and easy to move. Store in a sealed jar away from sunlight.

blooming salad

A salad of edible flowers can be beautiful and tasty.

In modern times, flowers have been used as a beautiful garnish for foods or salads. But now, as in times past, they are appearing in dishes for their flavor as well as their beauty.

Some flowers are similar to lettuce in not having much flavor, but many are very flavorful. The flowers of borage have a strong cucumber flavor; chive flowers add an onion flavor; bee balm has a minty lemon flavor; lemon thyme has the pungency and flavor of lemon; pot marigold flowers are tangy; tuberous begonias have a light lemon flavor; honeysuckle tastes like honey and pinks have a spicy clovelike flavor. Lavender is very pungent and should be added in small doses. Nasturtiums have beautiful flowers with little flavor, but their leaves are very spicy and can be substituted for ground pepper. Tulips have a crisp texture and are similar to peas, but taste a little sweeter. (Make sure you remove the pollen and stigma from the tulips before using as they do not taste good.) Violets, apple blossoms, lilacs and roses have a sweet floral taste, but each variety has a slightly different flavor. To avoid disappointment, you must smell and taste the flower before using it. The more fragrant the flower, the stronger the flavor.

Some edible flowers like chives, lavender and roses have hard centers that are not tasty. In these cases, only the petals are added to the salad, not the whole flower. A salad with flowers is a treat for the eyes as well as the palate.

flowers in ice cubes

Individual flowers frozen in ice cubes can make a drink sparkle and shine. Wash the flowers with lukewarm water and place each blossom in an individual ice cube compartment that is half full of water. Flowers float, so if you want the flower to be frozen in the middle of the cube, it has to be frozen first in a half-filled tray; add more water later to form the top half of the cube.

Edible flowers frozen in ice cubes are a treat for a summer party.

Party Cake

A birthday or party cake decorated with edible flowers and complete with a pond of swimming goldfish is a surprise for children and adults alike, and a fun activity for a birthday girl or boy to help make. Using a rectangular-shaped cake, cut out the center to the desired shape and insert an aluminum foil pan, a bowl or a jelly mold (as featured in the picture) which becomes a fish pond. The bottom of the fish pond can be covered with marbles or tiny white gravel. Fill the pond with tap water and allow it to sit for several hours until it has reached room temperature. A drop of blue food coloring can be added to the water, if you would like a colored pond. Next the cake should be frosted and decorated with fresh flowers. At the last minute, fish purchased at the pet store are added to the pond. Later we add the fish to our pond or to the kids' fish tank.

A pond complete with goldfish makes a funny birthday cake.

wear flowers

Here are some simple, quick and attractive ways for little girls to wear flowers:

Headbands, barrettes, combs and pins can all be decorated with garden flowers to wear to birthday parties, weddings or for any special occasion. Plain barrettes, combs and unadorned headbands can be purchased at most dime stores or drug stores. The best way to attach flowers to the ornaments is by winding thin, green floral or picture-hanging wire around them. The wire does not show, but holds the flowers gently in place. For dressy occasions, headbands can be covered with ribbon first or thin ribbons can be wrapped over the wire.

You can make floral hair ornaments a day ahead by leaving the stems long enough to keep refrigerated in water until you are ready to wear them. Then simply cut the stems and put them in your hair. I wear them for garden parties, summer dinners and even

Catie likes to pin sweet peas on her dress so she can enjoy their wonderful perfume all day long.

Rosebuds last all day when wired onto a barrette.

black-tie events. If you know what flowers you want to wear and have the materials close at hand, it should only take a few minutes to prepare. Flowers that dry naturally will last longer, such as a rose in bud, lavender, blue salvia, astilbe, celosia, delphiniums and larkspur. Long, spiky flowers such as butterfly bush, delphinium and astilbe are easy to bend around a headband. Since leaves wilt first, it is usually better to strip the leaves off the stem before attaching it to combs.

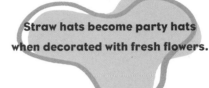

Straw hats become party hats when decorated with fresh flowers.

Straw hats are easily decorated with single flowers or clusters. The brim of the hat can be turned up and held with a decorated hat pin (the hat pin can also hold a flower). Fresh flowers that wilt quickly can be placed in several plastic floral tubes and arranged to cover the brim of the hat. The tubes can be tucked into the hat band, or attached with quick-dry glue. Velcro can also be sewed onto the hat so the tubes can be easily taken out to fill with water and to change the flowers. The tubes will then have to be hidden by leaves, a ribbon or a hat band. A florist trick is to soak a tiny ball of cotton in water and poke it into the center of a trumpet flower where it will not be seen but will add moisture to help the flower stay fresh.

Flowers that last for a long time without being in water and flowers that dry naturally (see everlastings, pages 68–70), need only be pinned in place without too much fuss. Wrap the brim with trailing vines that could hang down the back, place a nosegay on one side, or group astilbe together to imitate feathers rising from the crown. The hat could even be used for a centerpiece, hung on a wall or worn to a wedding. Fragrant flowers are a joy and should be used whenever possible.

Dressing up dolls with flowers is a creative activity for a child.

A headband, a hatband or a choker can be made by sewing individual flowers onto a ribbon. If you would like it to last for longer than a day or two, it can be dried in silica gel. One variation is to sew hydrangea flower petals onto a ribbon, accenting the middle with a few rosebuds, cornflowers, or other flowers that will dry naturally or last a few days without wilting. It is simple and quick to sew hydrangea petals on yard-long ribbon. Using a running stitch, small on the side with the flowers, large on the backside, give each flower one stitch. It will take approximately twenty minutes.

Pin a rosebud to the neck of a blouse, on the lapel of a jacket, popping out of a pocket, or tucked in a braid or ponytail. It will easily keep and, if fragrant, remind you of its presence all day. Try putting a fragrant flower in your pocket and the perfume will stay with you all day. The entrance to our house is covered with honeysuckle which is in full bloom in June and has sporadic blooms for the rest of the summer. Everyone who comes and goes through the front door is greeted by a wonderful fragrance all summer long. When I go out, I frequently pick a blossom and put it in my pocket to carry a little of the garden with me.

simple ideas for growing in the garden

Activities with children in the garden are endless. The following are a few projects that require little effort and bring quick results. They involve the ABC's of growth.

In teaching them, do not worry about perfection. It's the child's attention you want to capture, so every activity must be fun. As you play in the garden, they will find new activities. Add them to this list and share them with us. Here's a start:

1. Introduce a child to Nature's diversity: grow many different varieties of the same vegetables—red, pink and yellow tomatoes, giant and tiny pumpkins, speckled, yellow and pink corn (all good for popping).

2. Carve a child's name in the outer skin of a pumpkin when it is young and let them check the pumpkin from time to time. As the pumpkin grows larger, so will the name.

Prizewinner pumpkins can weigh several hundred pounds.

3. Try some of the unusual colored vegetables. They will make an interesting taste treat for the whole family: golden beets, rainbow corn, purple cabbage and 'Royal Burgundy' (purple pod beans that turn green when cooked—it must be magic!).

4. Help your child grow a large cucumber inside a narrow-necked glass bottle. Friends won't know how you did it. It is the same principle as ships in bottles. A baby cucumber can easily be slipped into the bottle while still growing on the vine. The bottle will act as a greenhouse holding and intensifying the heat of the sun, which could rot the cucumber if the bottle isn't shaded with cucumber leaves or old newspapers. Cut the cucumber from the vine when it has almost filled the bottle. To preserve it, you can pickle it right in the jar.

5. Measure a child against a mammoth sunflower when the sunflower is a little taller than the child. Wrap a ribbon around the stem to mark the height or draw a line with an indelible ink pen. The children will be surprised over the next few weeks to see how quickly the ribbon or the line rises over their heads.

Measuring kids against a sunflower will teach them about the miracle of growth.

A golden watermelon is a conversation piece to surprise garden visitors.

84

6. Spell out the child's name with plants: Leaf lettuce, parsley and dwarf marigolds are all good choices.

7. Grow a garbage garden from vegetable scraps rescued from the garbage pail. The next time you're peeling root vegetables—carrots, turnips, beets or parsnips, for example—cut the tops off leaving the foliage and an inch of the vegetable. Have your youngster get a plate and cover the shallow bottom with water. Set the vegetables in the water and place the plate in a sunny window to "see what will happen." Water will have to be added to the plate almost daily so the roots stay in water. In 2 to 3 weeks, a pretty garden of leafy greens will grow (they won't produce more vegetables).

8. Gather white flowers—mums, shasta daisies, cosmos, Queen Anne's lace—and put their stems in water colored with food dye. The stems of the flowers will take up the colored water and the flowers themselves will change from white to the color of the water.

crafts from gourds

The gourds used for craft projects should be the larger gourds that grow in round, pear and oblong shapes. They are sold as seeds under the names of 'Dipper', 'Pilgrim's Bottle', 'Calabash', 'Swan' and 'Hercules Club'. After they are harvested, they must be dried or cured for six months or more in a dark, warm place. When cured, the seeds will make a rattling sound as the gourd is shaken. Once cured, a gourd can be cut, carved, hollowed out, lacquered, varnished, painted or waxed.

If the gourd develops fungus on its shell, scrape it off and clean the shell with a disinfectant such as household bleach (mix the bleach with ten parts of water to one part of bleach).

Once the gourds have cured, soak them in boiling water to help remove the outer waxy skin which can easily be scraped off with a knife or stiff brush. Paint will not adhere to this waxy skin. When the gourds are still wet from their soaking, it is the easiest time to cut them into shapes for birdhouses.

If you prefer to paint them, lightly sand the gourd to prepare the surface so the paint will adhere. Poster or acrylic paints are perfect for gourd painting. Look at each gourd as an individual and let your imagination go wild. Gourds can be painted to look like round people (Santa is a favorite), animals or monsters. Gourds can even have designs burnt into them with a wood-burning needle.

Gourds can be decoratively painted and used as birdhouses.

'Dipper' and 'Birdhouse' gourds are easily made into low-cost wren houses. To make one, bore or cut a smooth, round hole the size of a quarter in the side of the large part of the gourd, then drill a smaller hole completely through the stem end. The small hole is for the hanging wire. Use a spoon handle or a dull knife to loosen the dried seeds and fibers so that they can be shaken out though the large hole. Finally, if you want to preserve the gourd for more than one season, paint the surface with shellac or polyurethane.

For more information write to the

American Gourd Society, Inc.
Box 274
Mount Gilead, Ohio 43338

the art of pressed flowers

Pressing flowers is an old, yet simple art. It can be done with a phone book or an inexpensive flower-pressing kit available in children's stores or craft stores.

Flowers with thin petals, such as pansies and violets, press easiest. Tulips and daffodils have thick petals that hold a lot of water, making them more difficult to press. All of the flowers that easily air-dry can be used. Pick the flowers in the morning after the dew has dried off. Lay them on a newspaper for a few hours to dry even further before you lay them in the pages of a phone book, or any heavy book.

Fat phone books are ideal for pressing flowers because their uncoated paper pages will soak all of the moisture out of the flowers. Leave the flowers in the book for six weeks to dry. The flowers can then be used to make bookmarks, pictures or greetings cards. They will be fragile when dry and difficult for children to move without breaking but if they break, they can be glued onto paper to appear whole.

Pressed flowers are pretty enough to frame.

To make a bookmark, cut a rectangular strip of paper approximately 2 inches wide and 6 inches long. Use colorful construction paper or rice paper, which can be found in an art supply store. Arrange the flowers on the bookmark in a design and glue the flowers down with a white glue applied carefully in small dots under each flower. After the glue dries, place the bookmark on the contact paper (also available from an art supply, hardware or crafts store) and cut a piece of clear contact paper large enough to cover the bookmark. Peel back the covering from the clear contact paper and place the bookmark on the adhesive side. Press and smooth it with your hand and fold the contact paper around the bookmark so it is completely enclosed. A hole can be punched in the top of the bookmark and a thin colorful ribbon looks beautiful tied through it.

Ferns and flowers are easy to press in thick telephone books.

A picture or a card can also be made using the same method, but cover only the front of the card or picture with the clear contact paper. The contact paper helps preserve the fragile flowers and protects them from humidity.

When choosing flowers for pressing, try any flowers you like. Here are a few that are easy and reliable and hold both their color and their shape:

Artemisia

Bleeding hearts

Daffodils

Geraniums

Hydrangea (whole blossoms or the individual petals)

Larkspur

Lavender

Pansies

Primroses

Roses

Salvia

Snowdrops

Violets

Drying assortments of foliage also make beautiful pressed projects. The types that work well are delicate cut leaf foliage such as ferns, bleeding hearts, lamb's ears, dusty miller, and various small-leaved varieties of herbs including thyme, sage and parsley.

a scavenger hunt

Gathering Nature's treasures in a scavenger hunt is a great adventure for kids. Scout your neighborhood and backyard to collect at least thirty different "treasures" to put on the list for the kids to find. With younger children I set up a display table with everything labeled so I am sure they know what they are looking for; and always remember to award prizes. A list in October might include the following:

a toadstool	an oak leaf
5 acorns	a nut
3 pinecones	a bird's nest
a red maple leaf	a bird's feather
a yellow leaf	a pine needle
a green leaf	a pinch of sand
red berries	mushrooms
a seedpod	a winged seedpod
a spider (that gets them every time!)	silver or white bark
a small white rock	a rose hip
brown bark	different broad evergreen leaves (azaleas, rhododendrons and holly)

Make sure the list includes at least thirty different things because the kids will find everything a lot faster than you do. They see where their friends found an object and they run instead of walk from place to place.

If the party is all boys and I have a few places where I would like the soil turned, I add worms, slugs, toads and any other slimy creature that comes to mind. They always love it, in spite of the loud groans. I assign points to each object based on the difficulty of finding it. For example, I award one point for each leaf of a different color, two points for a pinecone, five points for a worm and ten points for a bird's nest. The point system also keeps them hunting longer and helps those who cannot find the difficult objects to gain points in quantity that they miss in quality.

If you serve cookies baked in the shapes of frogs, mushrooms, butterflies and other wildlife, you will be the hit of the party.

Girls' Parties

Little girls love playing "dress up" for an afternoon tea party in the garden. Instead of tea, serve cold lemonade with flowers frozen in the ice cubes, and brownies decorated with candied flowers, all served on a table sprayed with a confetti of flower petals.

A lemonade party in the garden
becomes a festive occasion
when brownies are decorated
with edible flowers.

If you'd like to plan some activities, let the girls
make some candied flowers to take home (see pages
75–76) or decorate straw hats, headbands or barrettes
with real flowers (see pages 80–82).

Even making nosegays or miniature bouquets are
activities they love. If I have an especially full cutting
garden, I encourage them to cut their own flowers.
Otherwise, I cut the flowers before they arrive.

conclusion

Gardening with children reinforces strong family roots for the parents and provides a liberal education for the child. The rewards are great. The garden always gives back more than the gardener puts in. So the children can give gifts from your garden, flowers for the home and vegetables for the table to neighbors, relatives and friends.

Although at this time, my older children have little interest in gardens or gardening, I am not distressed, knowing that this too will pass. My youngest daughter, teetering into her teens, sees our cut flower garden as a potential for pocket money. Without any notice she sets up a flower stand outside the garden gate, selling bunches of cut flowers to passing cars and strollers. Fortunately, the more flowers are cut the more they grow.

I have great faith that a love of gardens will grow in my children's hearts from the seeds of their young memories. I have no fear that they too will be irresistibly drawn back to the garden. Time spent in the garden with an impressionable child is always a good investment in a child's future.

Teach children to smell flowers. They will be pleasantly surprised at the variety of different fragrances.

Children can never grow too
many pumpkins. This one is
called 'Baby Bear'.

4

fun and funny plants

Flowers and vegetables abound, each with their own unique personality, and most could easily be included here. All plants are interesting in their own way, although all are not easy to grow. Look at the pictures in this book and see what catches your and your child's fancy. The plants chosen are fun and easy for children to grow.

Each flower and vegetable is listed under its common name, and the flowers are cross-referenced by their botanical names, to avoid misunderstanding and to be scientifically correct. The botanical names may be difficult to remember and even harder to pronounce, but they are important. Botanical names are the same everywhere in the world, no matter what language is spoken. Occasionally, a plant has the same common name as its Latin name, zinnia for example. The system was founded by the Swedish botanist Carolus Linnaeus. Every known plant is first placed in a genus (the first Latin word), a group with similar characteristics, and is then further classified into a species (second Latin word), which identifies shared qualities of lesser importance. The common names are much easier to pronounce, but different flowers grown in different parts of the country often have the same common name. Using botanical names is the one way to be sure you receive the correct cultural information.

useful information
symbols and terms

Throughout this section, we have used symbols and terms. Here's what they mean:

Latin names of the flowers are in italic. Vegetables are listed only by their common names.

Phonetic pronunciation of the Latin name is in parentheses.

Common name of the flowers and vegetables comes first because it is the easiest way for a child to remember the plant's name. (Many of the flowers have more than one common name listed.)

The average hours of sun needed per day are listed by symbols; the first symbol is preferred, although the plant is adaptable to all conditions listed.

SUN
six hours or more of strong, direct sunlight per day

PART SHADE
three to six hours of direct sunlight per day

beans

Beans, surprisingly enough, can interest children whether they eat them or not. Here are some intriguing types:

Scarlet runner bean vines grow eight feet or more a season and continue to be covered with red flowers even as they produce green beans.

Yard-long beans will indeed grow that long if left on the vine.

Asparagus beans, sometimes called yard-long beans, are easy to grow. As their name indicates, they can grow to be almost three feet long. However, for the best flavor, pick and serve most of them before they reach 18 inches, while they are still very supple. Try letting the kids pick them and tie them in knots before steaming them. The fun is in the novelty of serving knotted beans, 18 inches long and hanging off the plate like spaghetti. They are quick to mature (50 days) and have a nutty flavor. They can be steamed, stir-fried or sautéed like snap beans.

'Royal Burgundy' beans are purple on the vine but become "magic beans" for children as they turn green when blanched in boiling water.

Scarlet runner bean is a fast-growing, decorative, flowering vine. Red flowers form all summer and produce bean pods until frost. Inside each pod are bright, neon-colored, scarlet beans that look like they could glow in the dark. This vine is very useful for making a tepee (see pages 42–43) or dressing a scarecrow (see pages 58–63).

butterfly bush,
Buddleia davidii
(BUD-lee-a da-VID-ee-eye)

Butterfly bushes, as their name implies, attract butterflies when they are in bloom. At summer's end the bushes are often covered with a dozen or more butterflies at the same time—a truly wonderful sight.

The bush's other common name is "summer lilac," a name that describes the flowers and their light fragrance. The flowers come in assorted colors from white to pink, lavender, orange and a reddish color.

The bushes grow quickly to 4 to 6 feet high each summer and bloom on new branches if they are cut to the ground at the end of winter. They do not require any special treatment and can be planted in average soil with good drainage.

Butterfly bushes are a magnet for butterflies when they bloom.

carrot

Carrots come in many sizes and shapes. 'Little Finger' is a baby carrot growing 3 1/2 inches long and less than 1 inch wide. 'Thumbelina' and 'Short 'n Sweet' are also small carrots with names that children can understand.

The tastiest carrots are usually sown in early spring, but later sowings extend the harvest into fall and winter.

Carrots grow best in soil that has been deeply worked and has had all the stones and sticks removed so the roots will grow straight. Good drainage is important to prevent rotting and disease. Wood ashes spread over the surface and raked into soil will provide a good source of potassium for sweeter-tasting carrots.

Carrots come in all sizes. Pictured here starting from the longest are 'Imperator', 'Toudo', 'Royal Chaternay', 'Goldinhart', 'Short 'n Sweet' and 'Little Finger'.

The smaller carrots will be ready for harvest in 60 to 70 days. Harvest them while they are still young for peak flavor, crunchiness and nutrition. The light, feathery foliage of carrots also works well in bouquets.

If you leave some carrots in the garden over the winter, they will produce lovely flowers and seeds for planting the following spring.

chinese lantern,
Physalis alkekengi
(fiss-a-lis al-ke-KEN-jee)

Chinese lanterns are perennial plants grown for their lantern-shaped orange pods. The papery pods serve to cover and protect the developing seeds.

In summer, the tiny, white flowers of Chinese lanterns come into bloom. Their dark green leaves hide the tiny white blossoms so if you do not look closely, you might miss them. After the blossoms have been pollinated by bees, hollow green seedpods form, and toward fall, they turn an orange-red color.

The green and orange puffs of Chinese lanterns resemble paper lanterns.

Chinese lantern plants will grow to about 2 feet tall. Cut the lanterns on long stems in the fall when they are just starting to turn from green to orange. Remove the leaves and tie several stems together and hang them upside down in a dry, well ventilated, dark place. It will take several weeks for the lanterns to dry properly. Stems should be hung upside down so the weight of the lanterns will be on the bottom and the stems will dry straight. When they are dry, they can be placed in a vase for a long-lasting, dried bouquet.

Average, well-drained soil is necessary for growing Chinese lanterns; no fertilizer is needed. In fact, plants may grow too rapidly if fed fertilizers or grown in rich soils. Buy started plants or grow them from seed following the directions on the package. Either way, you will have flowers and lanterns the first summer. Because these are rampant growers, you may wish to confine them in a separate garden area where they will not crowd neighboring plants.

101

cockscomb, *Celosia*
(se-LO-see-a)

Celosia is a Latin name that has also become a common name. Celosias are old-fashioned favorites for cutting and drying, perfect for holiday decorations. I use them to decorate evergreen wreaths.

The feathery plumes of celosia can be picked to use in dried-flower bouquets.

There are two distinct styles—the crested and the plumed. The crested varieties resemble a knobby rooster's comb and the plumed varieties look like silky feathers. Within each style there are short and tall varieties in a range of bold, crayonlike colors including red, orange, yellow and pink.

Some of the named varieties recommended are: 'New Look', a dwarf plant with intense scarlet plumes and deep bronze foliage, 'Jewel Box Red', an exceptional cultivar specially suited to Southern gardens, 'Fancy Plumes', 'Century', 'Floradale', and 'Castle'.

All celosias bloom midsummer to frost and are not fussy about soil. They are heat-loving plants that tolerate drought but are sensitive to both cold temperatures and root disturbances. Be sure to plant seeds outdoors after the soil has warmed.

If growing for dry flower bouquets, cut before the flower begins going to seed. Strip the leaves, wire the stem to give support, and follow the instructions on pages 68–70.

Celosias take 75 to 100 days to grow from seed before they are ready for picking.

four o'clock, *Mirabilis*
(mee-RAH-bi-lis)

'Four o'clocks' help teach children to tell time. The flowers open late each day, around four o'clock, and remain open all night and into the next day, closing in bright sun to protect themselves from scorching. On overcast days, when we all need a lift, they are in full bloom. Each plant may be a single color or have flowers of many different colors, usually white, red, rose, yellow and an occasional bicolor, in different combinations.

Four o'clock flowers open late in the day around four o'clock.

An old-fashioned tender perennial for frost-free areas and an annual for Northern gardens, four o'clocks sprout readily, bloom profusely and tolerate dust, soot, fumes and other pollutants, which makes them a perfect choice for a city gardener or a children's garden. Four o'clocks reseed themselves with enthusiasm and are very attractive to hummingbirds.

They will grow in poor or sandy soil. However, when given good soil and an occasional feeding, they are appreciative. Their roots form tubers that can be dug up in the fall and saved like the tubers of dahlias and begonias for planting again the next spring. The flowers bloom in 60 to 85 days from seed.

globe amaranth,
Gomphrena globosa
(gom-FREE-na glo-BO-sa)

Globe amaranth are everlasting flowers with papery, cloverlike blooms. They are available in the shimmering iridescent colors of white, pink, red, purple and orange on 1 1/2 - to 2-foot-tall plants. The dried red-and-white globe flowers look like Christmas decorations on miniature trees.

They tolerate drought and heat, but need water in extended periods. To speed germination, soak the seeds in lukewarm water for three or four days and then spread the wet, cottony seed mass thinly over the top of the soil. They bloom about 70 to 80 days after planting.

The button-shaped flowers of globe amaranth dry naturally in the garden and can be picked for winter bouquets.

gourds

Since ancient times gourds have been useful tools for mankind. In older civilizations they were dried and cut as dippers, storage containers and water flasks. Today they are used to make rattles and birdhouses, and can be decoratively painted (see pages 85–86).

To make utensils, types of gourds are used that have thin shells and a long growing season. They are sold under the names of 'Dipper', 'Pilgrim's Bottle', Calabash', 'Dolphin', 'Swan', and 'Hercules' Club'—the names pertaining to their shapes.

Large gourds are approximately 90 percent water and grow in round, pear and oblong shapes, as well as unusual or contorted shapes that make them suitable for craft projects. If you prefer straight necks, grow them on fences or trellises, to prevent their necks from curling.

Some gourds are grown for their "good looks." 'Turk's Turban' is a particular favorite because of its brilliant orange and yellow color and its interesting, turbanlike shape. The most popular gourd seed packets are the small fancy gourd mixes which include a colorful mix of yellow, orange, green and white fruits, some with stripes and bicolors, and a variety of shapes—like an apple, orange, pear, egg or bottle.

Children can scratch initials or designs into the skin of a young gourd and watch the designs grow with the gourd.

Gourds are ready to be harvested when their green color changes to tan and their shells feel hard. They should be harvested after frost, leaving 1 to 2 inches of stem on the fruit.

Gourds come in a variety of shapes and sizes. Pick your favorite from the pictures on the seed packets.

impatiens, touch-me-not, busy lizzy, patient plant, *Impatiens walleriana*

(im-PAY-shee-ens wo-la-ree-ah-na)

When impatiens seeds are ripe, the plants are poised to send them flying into the air. A child's touch can trigger their pop.

Impatiens are such popular plants that they have many nicknames. 'Busy Lizzy', 'Touch-me-not' and 'Patient Plant' are only a few. All of these nicknames describe the ripe seedpods that impatiently burst open when slightly touched. Their colors include white, red, pink, lilac and various bicolors.

'Rosette' hybrid impatiens have flowers that are double and look like miniature roses. 'Blitz' hybrids come in a wide variety of colors and are large-flowered (2 inches across), compact plants, 14 to 16 inches high. 'Super Elfin' hybrids are dwarf, uniform, low-spreading plants 10 to 12 inches in height. The 'Dazzler' hybrids have the widest array of colors with 2-inch flowers on 8-inch stems.

Impatiens like a rich well-drained soil with plenty of moisture during dry periods. Use slow-release fertilizers, low in nitrogen, to provide nutrients during the whole growing season. Impatiens bloom in 53 to 75 days from seed.

The Garden Speaks

Expressions have been borrowed from garden experiences for everything from nursery rhymes to common phrases. Here are a few of the most common:

"*cool as a cucumber*"

"red as a beet"

Your ears are like flowers—cauliflowers.

Mind your peas and cukes.

Q: What's the difference between a gardener and a billiard player?

A: One minds his peas and the other his cukes.

Peter, Peter, pumpkin eater.
Had a wife and couldn't keep her;
He put her in a pumpkin shell,
And there he kept her very well.

If wishes were horses,
Then beggars would ride.
If turnips were watches,
I'd wear one by my side.

What's in a Name?

The common names of flowers give clues to their personality. For example, impatiens were so named because they are "impatient," shooting their seed into the air the moment they are ripe.

Love-in-a-puff is aptly named, for inside each puffy seedpod are three jet-black seeds, each decorated with a white heart.

Black-eyed Susan is a yellow flower with a black center or eye.

Balloon flower has flower buds that look like blue, pink or white balloons before they open.

The names of flowers can be used to stretch the child's imagination. Introduce children to the flowers and let them see if they can tell a tall tale about how each flower got its name. They will probably guess right. Look through garden catalogues and you will be able to easily add to the following list:

Black-cycd Susan

Bleeding heart

Blue lace flower

Butterfly flower

Chinese lanterns

Cockscomb

Forget-me-not

Four o'clock

Kiss-me-over-the-garden-gate

Love-in-a-mist

Love-in-a-puff

Love-lies-bleeding

Moonflower

Obedience plant

Pincushion flower

Polka-dot plant

Snapdragon

Starflower

Strawflower

Touch-me-not

Winged everlasting

Vegetables have funny names, too, that children love, and they are also easy to remember. For a start, here is a list of vegetables with funny names. The children can make a story around the vegetable and how it got its name.

'French Breakfast' radish

'Green Goliath' broccoli

'Little Finger' carrot

'Pickalot Hybrid' cucumber

'Sweet Dream Hybrid' melon

'Burpless' cucumber

'Red Sails' loosehead lettuce

'Sweet Banana' pepper

'Turk's Turban' gourd

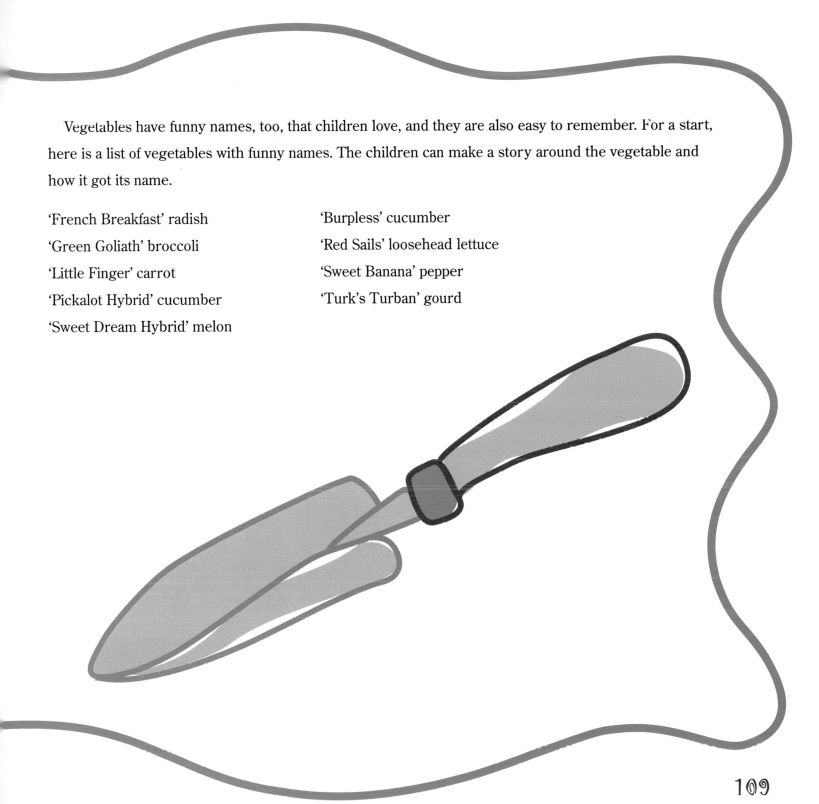

lamb's ears,
Stachys byzantina
(b i - z a n - T E E - n a)

Lamb's ears is a perennial plant grown for its furry, silvery leaves that beg to be petted. Encourage children to touch them. The leaves, when picked, dry naturally.

The tiny, pink flowers cover the top of 4- to 6-inch spikes and bloom from July through September. The leaves are arranged in low clumps, 6 to 12 inches high, and often spread to 24 inches wide.

Plant lamb's ears in a well-drained soil of average fertility. It is long-lived, neat and restrained in growth.

Divide the plant in the spring, after its fourth year of bloom, to rejuvenate.

The large, soft, silvery leaves of lamb's ears feel like a furry lamb.

love-in-a-puff,
Cardiospermum
(kar-dee-o-SPERM-um)

'Love-in-a-puff' was a popular vine in colonial days that is all but forgotten today. It is a delicate vine, with small, green leaves and white flowers tiny as pinheads. The excitement of this vine is in the 3-inch green, round, papery puffs, that protect the seeds as the flowers fade. When the puffs turn brown, they can be popped like small balloons to reveal three round, black seeds, each with its own perfect white heart. The hearts form where the seed attaches to the pod.

I showed this to my youngest daughter, Catie, one morning in early August. I thought she did not seem quite as excited as I was about the unusual and beautiful seeds, until I returned later in the day to discover the vine completely stripped of every green puff. She brought the whole neighborhood to search for more black seeds with hearts. But in their enthusiasm they had picked the puffs too early in the green stage, and found only green unripened seeds. Luckily, the vines continued to flower. A few weeks after Catie and her friends had stripped the vine, it was again covered with green puffs.

The black seeds of love-in-a-puff have small white hearts on them.

The seeds are easy to grow in average soil. The plants frequently reseed themselves each year without help from the gardener and are never a nuisance. Since the seeds are so much fun to collect, once you buy a pack of seeds you can have it forever, as you can collect them year after year. I simply push the seed into the ground, covering them lightly with fine soil, where I want them to grow.

money plant, "silver dollar plant," honesty, *Lunaria*

(loon-AH-ree-a)

What child wouldn't love to grow money on a tree? The money plant blooms with blue flowers in the spring and forms silvery, translucent seedpods that resemble silver dollars in midsummer. As it is a biennial, the seeds planted the first year will not bloom until the second year.

The money plant is not a fussy grower and it thrives in ordinary soil. They are easily grown; when planted in June they bloom and produce seeds by the following summer. Although they are biennial, they self-sow prolifically and may become a nuisance. When cutting for drying, cut as soon as the green fades from the seed heads, then bring them inside to protect them from the rain and the wind. Do not worry if the silver dollars look spotted and dirty. This is only a protective covering that can be rubbed off lightly with your fingers.

The money plant has silvery seeds that look like coins.

moonflower,
Ipomoea alba
(i-po-MEE-a AL-ba)

Moonflowers light up the garden at dusk and into the night. These vigorous annual vines climb up to 15 feet high in one summer with large, moon-shaped, very fragrant, pure white flowers, 5 to 6 inches across. The flowers open early in the evening and close before noon the following day. However, if the day is overcast and dark, they are fooled into staying open later. Their heart-shaped leaves are large, reaching up to 8 inches. The stems can be prickly, and are covered with fine hairs. So be careful when handling the vine.

They are also quick-twining vines, and the stems can complete a circle around their host in three hours. Buds can be cut and used in an evening flower arrangement, but will be gone by morning. Moonflower's sweet, heavenly scent is concentrated in the oil between the central bands inside the open flower. The perfumed oil attracts night-flying moths which fertilize the flowers. Each flower lasts one night but the buds come fast and furious until frost.

Before planting the seeds, chip the seed coat opposite the seed scar and soak them overnight to speed the number and rate of germination. They are difficult to transplant and easy to sow directly where you want them to grow when the soil is warm. The flowers will bloom in approximately 90 days from when the seeds are sown. (Follow the same directions for growing morning glories.)

Moonflowers open at night and perfume the air. If you watch the flowers in the late afternoon, you may see one of them open.

morning glory,
Ipomoea purpurea
(i-po-MEE-a pur-PEWR-ree-a)

Morning glories can be a wonderful backdrop to a flower garden. The flowers bloom in pink, blue or white. 'Heavenly Blue', with 4- to 5-inch sky-blue flowers, is one of the tallest morning glories, and 'Early Call' with mixed colors is one of the shortest. 'Scarlett O'Hara' has crimson-carmine flowers, and 'Pearly Gates' has shining white flowers.

Morning glories can be planted at the base of sunflowers after they have been growing a few weeks, as the sunflower can support the weight of the vine. They are most popular growing up drain-pipes, mailbox posts and any other structure in need

Morning glories open with the first light and close in the early evening.

of some sprucing. In fact, they can be planted just about anywhere to camouflage unsightly buildings or trash bins. They can be trained to grow over hedges, climbing roses or large bushes to make them appear to be flowering. They can also be trained to grow down from large pots or window boxes, scramble along the ground over a dead tree trunk, or even help brighten up hillsides or barren land. They will not cause any damage to their host if grown where frost stops their travels. Almost everyone can find a place to grow them.

CAUTION: All parts of morning glory vines are poisonous, if eaten.

The seeds have a hard shell that makes it difficult for the plant embryo to break through. To speed germination, soak the seeds in water at room temperature several hours before planting to soften the outer shell, or score the outer shell with a sharp knife to allow the embryo to break through. Higher germination will result from either method or both combined.

The seeds can be planted outside early but they will not grow until the soil and air temperature are consistently warm. The plant needs some protection from strong winds, and a trellis, string or a fence to wind around as it climbs. Morning glories have tendrils that reach out and twine around netting or trellises, pulling themselves up. Do not overwater; let topsoil dry out between watering.

Morning glories prefer poor, well-drained soil and flower more if they are not fertilized. They self-sow easily and bloom in approximately 75 days.

pumkins

Whether giant or tiny, pumpkins have always been a favorite of children. 'Jack-be-little' pumpkins are miniatures, just 3 inches across and 2 inches high. These vines can be grown on a fence, tepee or trellis and each vine will produce 6 or 7 pumpkins in approximately 95 days. Small children, like my neighbor's four-year-old, enjoy picking and carrying these tiny pumpkins around.

'Lumina'(vp) is grown for its strangeness. On the outside, it a ghostly white pumpkin, although the inside remains orange. Their size, 8 to 10 inches across, makes them perfect for face painting or carving. They mature in 80 to 90 days.

'Baby Bear' is not quite a miniature, with individual pumpkins 6 inches across and 3 to 4 inches high, but it is an easy size for young children to carry. It is ready to harvest in approximately 105 days.

Of course pumpkins are best known in larger sizes, and the biggest is 'Prizewinner', which takes a little longer, 120 days, to grow big. If you want to show off or enter competitions, allow only one pumpkin to grow on a vine. Begin pinching off all new flowers after one pumpkin has a good start and leave it plenty of room to grow. Four-hundred-pound pumpkins have been grown this way, although when grown normally, they usually average 80 to 100 pounds.

Follow the directions on the individual seed pack for whichever pumpkin you choose to grow. In general, pumpkins should be harvested when the rinds are hard and are a deep solid orange; they must be harvested before they are injured by the first heavy frost.

Pumpkins come in all sizes. They can be large enough to bake into a pie or carve into a jack-o'-lantern or tiny enough to hold in your hand.

All pumpkin seeds are edible and nutritious. Some have seed coats and some are "naked." To prepare the seeds for eating, scoop them out of the pumpkin and wash them lightly to separate them from the pulp. Spread the seeds on paper towels or plates and let them dry for a few days in a warm, dry, well-ventilated place.

radish

The patience of children is minimal so radishes are the perfect vegetable for the children's garden. They are ready to pick and eat in 22 to 30 days. Their speedy growth keeps children interested although, be warned, many children do not like to eat them. However, they will be happy to feed them to adults.

The assorted radishes in the picture include 'French Breakfast', 'Cherry Belle' and 'White Icicle'.

Radishes vary greatly in color and size underground while remaining identical above the soil. If seeds of different varieties are mixed together before they are planted, the children will be surprised by what they pull out of the ground. A good mix could include 'Cherry Belle' with its round red balls, 'White Icicle', descriptively named, 'French Breakfast', long and red, and 'Easter Egg Hybrid', which are oval-shaped in reddish purple, lavender, pink, rose, scarlet and white.

Plant radishes in a loamy soil, free of rocks and stones that can cause misshapen roots. The usual way to plant radishes is to sow them in double rows 6 inches apart with a foot between each set of rows. Sow seeds $1/3$ inch deep with three seeds per inch of row. When the plants are half grown, thin them so there are 12 to 18 plants per foot of row.

snapdragons, *Antirrhinum*
(an-ti-RY-num)

Snapdragons are so named because their blossoms resemble open mouths. If squeezed where they hinge, they snap open and shut like a miniature jaw, and children are fascinated by them. These colorful old-fashioned favorites are available in white, scarlet, rose, crimson, pink, yellow, orange and even bicolors.

Depending on the variety, plants grow from 8 to 36 inches tall and bloom heavily in early summer. If the faded spikes are cut off, they continue to flower all summer, but with smaller flower stalks and fewer blooms. Snapdragons are perennials in frost-free areas and can bloom with light frost in northern climates. In mild climates, plants bloom from early winter until summer.

Snapdragons do not like heavy soils, as their roots are very fine. In heavy soils, be sure to add lots of compost. They grow best in cool weather, moderately rich soil, in either sun or partial shade. The seeds need light to germinate and will bloom in approximately 53 to 65 days.

The flowers of snapdragons are hinged like a dragon's mouth and will move up and down if gently squeezed.

119

spider plant,
Cleome
(klee-O-mee)

These rapid-growing flowers will be 3 to 5 feet tall when they bloom in purple, white or burgundy. Spider plants have seedpods that develop and dangle, like spider legs, under big, airy flower clusters. When seeds are ripe, the pods burst open. A child's touch will trigger the pod to open.

On bright sunny days, the flower petals curl up, then open again as the coolness of evening approaches. Even curled, the flowers are showy. This free-flowering plant makes wonderful long-lasting cut flowers, and when kept out of direct sun, the petals stay open all the time.

When grown in a row, the plants create a temporary hedge 3 feet wide and are useful to screen out an unsightly area. If planted at the back of a small garden, four plants are enough to cover a 9-by-3-foot area. Plants can be leafless and leggy at the bottom, so it is best to plant in front of them.

When cutting for bouquets, be careful to hold the flower on the main stem between branches. A thorn is located at every place where a flowering branch joins the stem. The leaves and stems are sticky to the touch and flowers have a pungent, lemon fragrance.

The seedpods of the spider plant dangle under the flower like the legs of a spider.

'Pink Queen', 'Purple Queen', 'Snow Queen', 'Helen Campbell' are all popular varieties that produce large, airy, delicate flowers.

Spider plant tolerates heat and drought. They can be sown directly outside after all danger of frost is past. The seedpods that form directly under the flower, while the flower is still blooming, add some interest to the flowers and need not be removed. You can remove faded flowers to help the plant branch and produce more flowers.

However, cleome are long flowering even while prolifically producing seeds. Whether you cut off spent flowers or not, the flowers will bloom until killed by hard, prolonged frost. Each individual flower lasts for several weeks. The plant frequently reseeds, but the seedlings may revert in color and appear weedy. Spider plants can be grown next to a fence and tied for support. They should be spaced two feet apart and will flower in approximately 60 to 70 days.

spaghetti squash

Spaghetti squash is a popular type of winter squash with spaghettilike flesh. Children are fascinated by the strangeness of scraping out the noodlelike strands of squash. When preparing spaghetti squash for the table, punch one or two small holes in the fruit with a metal skewer and then boil the whole squash for 30 minutes or bake it for an hour. When the surface yields to pressure, it is done. Cut the squash lengthwise, scoop out the seeds and discard them. Remove the spaghetti strands by dragging a fork back and forth across the surface, then put them in a bowl and fluff lightly.

Cooked strands may be served like regular pasta, tossed with butter and grated parmesan cheese or topped with tomato sauce. They can also be chilled and added to salads.

The squash are ready for harvest when they have turned from green to yellow. At that time, they are about 8 to 10 inches long and weigh 3 to 6 pounds.

Spaghetti squash should be harvested with an inch of stem attached to the fruit and cured outdoors in a sunny spot for about a week. It should then be stored in a cool, dry place.

When spaghetti squash is cooked, it can be scooped out with a fork and it separates into strands that look like spaghetti.

strawflower,
Helichrysum bracteatum
(hee-li-KRY-sum brak-tee-AH-tum)

Strawflowers are a popular everlasting flower for winter bouquets. They are available in a wide assortment of bold and unusual colors including white, yellow, pink, orange, red, gold and crimson. The double-petaled, daisylike flowers practically dry on the plant, and they hold their bright colors when dried. The flower's petals feel like paper or straw, thus the name. A perennial from Australia, it flowers easily from seed the first year.

Strawflowers are easy to grow in average, well-drained soil, and they despise soils that are too rich or too wet. To dry them, cut the flowers before the center petals open and their pollen shows. Depending on the variety, they will be anywhere from 16 to 36 inches tall and will bloom in 50 to 85 days from planting.

**Strawflowers feel and look
like paper flowers.**

123

sunflowers,
Helianthus annuus
(hee-lee-ANTH-us AN-ew-us)

Sunflowers flaunt their sunny personalities. I defy you to look at them without smiling. The best-known sunflowers have large, daisylike single or double flowers that sprout rapidly to tower above everything else in the garden, which is what makes them a favorite of children. What else can grow 12 feet in little over three months? 'Mammoth' sunflowers quickly achieve very impressive heights and intrigue children in the process. Lined up, standing at attention against a fence, a regiment of sunflowers makes a decorative screen. Two of the largest varieties are 'Mammoth', and 'D 131 Hybrid'.

The 'Mammoth' sunflower, when planted at an entrance, is as imposing as the guards at Buckingham Palace. Whether standing at attention or with heads bowed, they mesmerize children of all ages. The year we grouped a dozen along the driveway, a neighbor stopped me to say they made her smile every time she passed by. The 'Mammoth' is the one variety of sunflower that is a must in any children's garden.

With their speedy growth, sunflowers become the perfect yardstick to mark the height of your child. Start when the sunflower is a head above your child. Tightly tie a ribbon around the stem of the sunflower to mark the child's height. As the sunflower grows, the ribbon will rise higher and higher above the child's head, emphasizing its speedy growth and gigantic size.

124

A sunflower is more than just a pretty face. Their edible seeds are great roasted or ground into sunflower butter. The seeds should be harvested when the flower petals have fallen. Birds love sunflower seeds, and you can leave the seeds to ripen on the flower head for the birds to enjoy. To save the seeds, chop off the whole flower head with a foot of stem and take it inside to dry. The head should be hung upside down in a dry room. When the seeds are dry, rub your hand across the surface and the seeds will come out. Each seed is protected by a white and black striped hull. The seeds can be eaten immediately after the hull is removed or they can be stored in an airtight container and later enjoyed as a nutritious snack or used to feed the birds in winter.

Other varieties such as 'Color Fashion' (to 5 feet) and 'Teddy Bear' (to 2 feet) are grown for their ornamental value and not their seed.

All sunflowers grow rapidly, sprouting in two to three weeks if the temperature is warm (between 68 and 86 degrees Fahrenheit). There is no need to start the seeds indoors unless you want a quick growing seed for an indoor project (see pages 12–13).

Plant the seeds in the garden after all danger of frost is past. They prefer light, dry, well-drained soil and they tolerate high heat. Water them only during a prolonged drought. Little or no fertilizer is needed unless the soil is very poor. Plant two or three seeds together and then thin to one every 2 to 4 feet as specified on the seed packet. Depending on how warm it is, and the variety of sunflower, they will flower in 55 to 75 days.

Giant sunflowers tower over children by summer's end.

zinnias, *Zinnia*
(ZIN-ee-a)

Zinnias have all the attributes children love in flowers. They are easy to grow, bloom in bright primary colors, and the more they are cut the more they bloom. 'Zenith Mixed' is a variety with giant, cactus-flowered blooms 6 inches across on 2 1/2-foot stems. 'Candy Cane Mixed' has smaller double flowers, 4 inches across, that bloom with bright pink, rose or cherry stripes on white. There are so many zinnias to choose from that you cannot go wrong.

The flat flowers of zinnias act as landing pads for butterflies.

Any well-drained garden soil, supplemented with a slow-release fertilizer, will grow zinnias. Seedlings require frequent watering but established plants will tolerate dry spells. Cut off any dead flowers, and the plants will bloom longer.

Zinnias need warm soil to germinate and will rot in the soil if planted before the soil is warm. The flowers are fairly quick to bloom, usually in about 55 days.

The Garden's Timekeepers

The blossoms of moonflowers and morning glories open only for a day. However, buds continuously form and masses of flowers are produced from midsummer to frost. Moonflowers, as their name implies, open as the sun starts to set, around 5 P.M., and close the next morning just after dawn. On a cloudy day, they often stay open until mid-morning. Morning glories open with the morning light and close midday if it is hot and sunny, but stay open all day if it is cloudy and pleasant. If you are patient, it is possible to watch them open, as long as you do not turn your back. Each flower puffs first, so it is easy to pick out the ones that are ready to open. They begin to quiver right before they open.

When the opening of moonflowers has been recorded on film, the whole process has taken seven or eight minutes from the time they begin to quiver until they are fully open. (The puffed moonflower can also be picked and put in water to open indoors.) To catch the show, you will need to check the vine frequently starting around five o'clock to see if there is any activity. Once you find the time they open, it's easy to invite prompt friends and their children for the next afternoon's show. The time will not vary much from day to day unless the weather is dark, overcast and nasty, in which case the flowers might not open. For those who rise at dawn, it is also possible to watch the morning glories open in the morning.

This is another of the mysteries of Nature. Even botanists debate what causes the flowers to open when they do. Most believe the flower opening is triggered by the amount of light present.

index